✔ **W9-AHG-818**

Dr. Ackerman's Book of
Great Danes

LOWELL ACKERMAN DVM

BB-116

Overleaf: A regal-looking Great Dane owned by Lois Ostrowski.

The author has exerted every effort to ensure that medical information mentioned in this book is in accord with current recommendations and practice at the time of publication. However, in view of the ongoing advances in veterinary medicine, the reader is urged to consult with his veterinarian regarding individual health issues.

Photographers: William Charles Anderson, Animal Attitudes, Greg DeMaria, Janet L. DeMaria, Sasha DeMaria, Christine Filler, Isabelle Francais, Peter Langham, Robert Lavin, Oren Marom, Vince Serbin, Catherine Woods.

The presentation of pet products in this book is strictly for instructive purposes only; it does not necessarily constitute an endorsement by the author, publisher, owners of dogs portrayed, or any other contributors.

© 1996 by LOWELL ACKERMAN DVM

Distributed in the UNITED STATES to the Pet Trade by T.F.H. Publications, Inc., One T.F.H. Plaza, Neptune City, NJ 07753; distributed in the UNITED STATES to the Bookstore and Library Trade by National Book Network, Inc. 4720 Boston Way, Lanham MD 20706; in CANADA to the Pet Trade by H & L Pet Supplies Inc., 27 Kingston Crescent, Kitchener, Ontario N2B 2T6; Rolf C. Hagen Inc., 3225 Sartelon St. Laurent-Montreal Quebec H4R 1E8; in CANADA to the Book Trade by Vanwell Publishing Ltd., 1 Northrup Crescent, St. Catharines, Ontario L2M 6P5 ; in ENGLAND by T.F.H. Publications, PO Box 15, Waterlooville PO7 6BQ; in AUSTRALIA AND THE SOUTH PACIFIC by T.F.H. (Australia), Pty. Ltd., Box 149, Brookvale 2100 N.S.W., Australia; in NEW ZEALAND by Brooklands Aquarium Ltd. 5 McGiven Drive, New Plymouth, RD1 New Zealand; in Japan by T.F.H. Publications, Japan—Jiro Tsuda, 10-12-3 Ohjidai, Sakura, Chiba 285, Japan; in SOUTH AFRICA by Lopis (Pty) Ltd., P.O. Box 39127, Booysens, 2016, Johannesburg, South Africa. Published by T.F.H. Publications, Inc.

MANUFACTURED IN THE
UNITED STATES OF AMERICA
BY T.F.H. PUBLICATIONS, INC.

CONTENTS

DEDICATION

To my wonderful wife Susan and my three adorable children, Nadia, Rebecca, and David.

PREFACE

Keeping your Great Dane healthy is the most important job that you, as an owner, can do. Whereas there are many books available that deal with breed qualities, conformation, and show characteristics, this may be the only book available dedicated entirely to the preventative health care of the Great Dane. This information has been compiled from a variety of sources and assembled here to provide you with the most up-to-date advice available.

This book will take you through the important stages of selecting your pet, screening it for inherited medical and behavioral problems, meeting its nutritional needs, and seeing that it receives optimal medical care.

So, enjoy the book and use the information to keep your Great Dane the healthiest it can be for a long, full, and rich life.

Lowell Ackerman DVM

BIOGRAPHY

D r. Lowell Ackerman is a world-renowned veterinary clinician, author, lecturer, and radio personality. He is a Diplomate of the American College of Veterinary Dermatology and is a consultant in the fields of dermatology, nutrition, and genetics. Dr. Ackerman is the author of 34 books and over 150 book chapters and articles. He also hosts a national radio show on pet health care and moderates a site on the World Wide Web dedicated to pet health care issues (**http://www.familyinternet.com/pet/pet-vet.htm**).

BREED HISTORY

THE GENESIS OF THE MODERN GREAT DANE by Jill Evans

T he European wild boar of long ago was a huge, bristly, bad-tempered beast with sharp tusks, weighing some 400 lbs. This animal regularly smashed  through dense forests, endangering people and decimating the local fauna. In the Middle Ages, aristocrats considered it great sport to "bag" thousands of wild boar in huge hunts.

Facing page: It is believed that the early ancestors of the Great Dane were giant, extremely strong dogs that were used to hunt wild boar in medieval Europe.

One such hunt, held in the Reinhard Forest area north of Frankfurt in 1563, captured nearly 2600. Accompanying the titled hunters on horseback were troops of the local villagers acting as beaters and packs of several hundred giant dogs of great agility, courage, strength, and perseverance. These dogs were kept in kennels and were frequently exchanged between princely estates in England, Germany, and possibly even Denmark. It's generally accepted that those mediaeval boarhounds are probably the ancestors of today's Great Dane. For the hunt, they often wore protective padded coats reinforced with whalebone, and their ears were cropped short so that they wouldn't be torn off by the angry boar or ripped in the forest's underbrush. After their dangerous excursions, some of the survivors were even cherished as housedogs. Count Philipp the Generous of Hessen was reported to keep some of his English imports "in the room with him at all times." He was particularly fond of a young dog called Weckuff, which was "white with a red spot on the ear and hind legs." The largest and best of these dogs wore gilded collars lined with velvet and were known as Kammerhunde

(chamber dogs), and the second best had collars of silver and were called Liebhunde (beloved dogs). The forebears of these fabled "Hatzrueden" are lost in antiquity, but dogs of similar appearance are found in artworks, coins, and the like from almost all over the world going back to time immemorial. Some of the earliest Egyptian tomb carvings (about five thousand years old) are of dogs remarkably like the Great Dane.

Those boarhounds of the middle ages were not all of one type according to paintings and tapestries of the time. Some were coarse, wire-haired dogs with fringed ears, and some were smooth-haired and had fairly pointed muzzles and houndy ears. Others were more like enormous terriers in appearance, and still others were very much in between in conformation — a smooth coat, heavy head, substantial body, square muzzle, and erect ears cropped very short — in other words, very much like the Danes first registered in England and Germany in the late 1800s. All were giants, and their colors ran the gamut of what appears in modern Danes and then some. Nobody really knows what breeds were mixed to produce these dogs, but there is conjecture that the extinct Irish

Greyhound, rough-coated "Mastins," hound-like "Alaunts," the bulky Tibetan Mastiff, and ancient Assyrian "battle-dogs" made contributions, along with hairier heavy breeds like the Molossian Hound of antiquity. The harlequin pattern is likely a donation from the long-gone Egyptian Greyhound.

Dane predecessors were used not only for chasing the wild boar but also hunted wolves, wild cattle, and stag. In Roman times, as well as later, they were used as war dogs, like Lord Cadogens's Great Dane shown in the tapestry of Marlborough's siege of Blenheim in 1704. The Romans also staged spectacles where huge dogs were pitted in fights against each other or animals such as bears. In Sweden and Denmark, tall dogs, "usually a light slaty-blue," were used in pairs to assist elk-finders. Dane-like dogs have also been used throughout the ages for gentler pursuits, such as to pull carts and, of course, to act as watchdogs. The story goes that they will let an intruder in, but not out unless given an okay by the owner.

As time passed, the wild boar became scarce, and boarhound packs were not needed anymore; the last rather coarse example was sold in 1876 in Germany. Even earlier, in 1800, Sydenham Edwards had written that the more refined members of this breed were used as carriage dogs to precede the entourage of the noble and wealthy. Only the most exalted employed

This group of Danes owned by Janet DeMaria models a variety of common coat color varieties—early Danes displayed these colors and more!

the "Danish Dog," while the coach dog for the less important was the Dalmatian, "the humble attendant of the servants and horses." The Dane was described as up to 31 inches high in conformation between the Greyhound and Mastiff and colored "sandy-red or pale fallow, with often a blaze of white on the face." A beautiful variety called the harlequin Dane had a "finely marked coat, with large and small spots of black, gray, liver-color, or sandy-red, upon a white

This Great Dane, owned by Joan Demers, displays the distinctive markings of a harlequin. Nineteenth century harlequins added sophistication to the processions of the social elite.

ground; the former often has tan-colored spots about the face and legs." Edwards adds, "I certainly think no equipage can have arrived at its acme of grandeur until a couple of harlequin Danes precede the pomp."

Another use for a Dane-like dog in Cuba and "Terra-Firma," was a "drover," or cattle-dog, described long ago by the British Colonel H. Smith. He considered them to be related to the feral dog of San Domingo, a wild representative of the Dane family. This native of the Western Hemisphere had the shape of a Dane but was wolf-colored with a black spot over each eye and had a rough coat. Col. Smith's description of its use follows:

We have often witnessed, when vessels with livestock arrive in our West India colonies, and the oxen are hoisted out by a sling passed round the base of their horns, the great assistance they afford to bring them to land. For, when the ox first suspended by the head is lowered, and allowed to fall into the water, men generally swim and guide it by the horns; but at other times this service is performed by one or two dogs, who, catching the bewildered animal by the ears, one on each side, force it to swim in the direction of the landing-place, and instantly release their hold when they feel it touches the ground, for then the beast naturally walks up the shore.

The development of the modern pure-bred Great Dane began about the middle of the 19th century, which also saw the advent of competitive dog shows in England and on the Continent. These grew enormously, and in 1887, the Stuttgart show had an entry of 300 Danes. A preliminary standard for the breed had been drawn up in Germany in 1800 where its popularity may have been influenced by the fact that the Chancellor, Prince Otto von Bismarck (born in 1815) was a great fancier and had owned several Danes from his early youth onward, the most famous of which was a blue dog called Tyras. Later in the century, the Dane was adopted as Germany's "National Dog," which discarded its various names in favor of Deutsche Doggen (German Mastiff). Strangely, in France, the name Dogue Allemand is used now, a direct translation of the German, while the French name Grand Danois (Great Dane) is only used in Scandinavia and Quebec. Italy calls the breed the Alano, a legacy of the Alaunt?

In England, Great Dane breeding records can be traced back to a bitch whelped in 1830 called Lukey's Old Bob-Tailed Countess. Interestingly enough, Mr. Lukey was better known for his Mastiff breeding, and there is a "Lukey's Countess" in a Mastiff pedigree of that same time. Great Danes were being used

The Great Dane as we know it today began to emerge and develop in 19th century Europe.

then to develop the Mastiff, and there is some indication that the cross worked both ways.

The world's first Great Dane Club was formed in England in about 1883. Next came the German Deutsche Doggen-Club in 1888, followed a year later by the Great Dane Club of America, whose members had been importing mainly from Germany. Unfortunately, many of the earliest imports from around 1880 were described as being "a bad-tempered lot" and resulted in the breed being banned from shows for several years. By the time the GDCA was formed, the "Apollo of dogs" had developed the gentle demeanor he was supposed to have.

A group of German admirers, who met in Berlin to set up the Deutsche Doggen-Club, must be given credit for their thoroughness and persistence in setting a written standard for the breed, selectively developing pure-bred Danes toward the ideal, and keeping detailed records, complete with pictures, of their progress. At that time, the dogs in the north had been heavy, coarse, and aggressive, while the southern variety was slender, elegant, and somewhat more timid. Once the standard was set between the two types, only prize-winners could be registered in the stud book. Among the pioneering men was Max Hartenstein of Plauen, in the east, who had owned and bred many prize-winners beginning in 1874, although few were ever registered. Another was Edward Messter of Nill, in the north, and

his brindle dog Nero I 609, whelped in 1876. Nero I 609 is considered the principal progenitor of the modern Great Dane because nearly all pedigrees of all colors eventually lead back to him. The Berliner, Fritz Kirschbaum mustn't be overlooked. Not only did this man breed generations of outstanding Danes, but he was a conscientious and hardworking stud book chairman in the earliest days, a respected international judge who even traveled to the USA in 1908, and the contributor of many valuable articles containing advice still pertinent today!

In 1895, the Prince of Wales (who was to become King Edward VII) asked that ear-cropping be discontinued. Although no such law was passed, the Kennel Club agreed that no cropped dog could be shown or registered, which was a big blow to Dane breeders. However, some die-hards rallied and countered by breeding Danes with neat, small, expressive ears that would not detract from the "look of dash and daring" called for in the British standard. Also in the late 19th century, England lost many dogs to a rabies scare and, for some time before World War I, had been importing outstanding stock from the Continent and

This pair of Laurel Danes harlequins shows how coat color continues to be passed down through the generations.

breeding to their long-established British lines with great success. Great Danes were no exception.

After WWI, an enormous effort was necessary to revitalize Great Danes everywhere that had suffered greatly from food shortages and other exigencies of war. Some obviously purebred Danes were found wandering loose in Germany and were rescued. If they passed muster from a panel of judges, they were deemed findling (foundlings) and accepted for conditional registration, often producing superbly in justification of their unknown heritage. Hard times in Germany continued into the twenties when its horrendous inflation began. Curiously, this

was a defining point for the breed when a spectacular family of nearly perfect and prepotent Danes arrived at the von der Saalburg kennels of Karl Färber in Bad Homburg. The mating of the brindle bitch Fauna Moguntia, of the elegant and tightly bred Hansa line, to the golden-fawn dog Ch. Bosko vd Saalburg, a descendant of the beautiful fawn Ch. Primas vd Rheinschanze, produced the glorious brindle Ch. Dolf vd Saalburg in 1924, who could probably hold his own in the show ring even now. The legacy of these Danes throughout the world is incalculable and has set type in all colors to the present day.

MIND & BODY

**PHYSICAL AND BEHAVIORAL TRAITS
OF THE GREAT DANE**

The Great Dane is a dog of courage and spirit. While these qualities can be attributed to many different breeds, the Great Dane possesses a unique amalgam of these Teutonic virtues. The Dane must be friendly and dependable with humans. The size of his mighty frame

and the size of his heart are compatible—he is a dog of great character, noble in expression, and soft of heart.

Facing page: A dog of this size must have a big heart! This friendly fawn Dane says, "Pleased to meet you!" Owned by Richard E. and Jane B. Farmer.

CONFORMATION AND PHYSICAL CHARACTERISTICS

This is not a book about show dogs, so information here will not deal with the conformation of champions or how to select one. The purpose of this chapter is to provide basic information about the stature of the Great Dane and qualities of its physical nature.

Clearly, beauty is in the eye of the beholder. Since standards come and standards go, measuring your dog against

Although all purebred Great Danes will resemble the breed standard, the Danes shown in conformation should be the ones that come closest to being ideal representatives of the breed.

some imaginary yardstick does little for you or your dog. Just because your dog isn't a show champion doesn't mean that he or she is any less of a family member, and just because a dog is a champion doesn't mean that he or she is not a genetic time bomb waiting to go off.

When breeders and those interested in showing Great Danes are selecting dogs, they are looking for those qualities that match the breed "standard." This standard, however, is of an imaginary Great Dane and it changes from time to time and from country to country. Thus, the conformation and physical characteristics that pet owners should concentrate on are somewhat different and much more practical.

The Great Dane combines dignity, power, and elegance in its giant frame. Male Great Danes are usually at least 30 inches (76 cm) in height (at the withers), and females are usually at least 28 inches (71 cm). The average approximate weight for males is 130 pounds (60 kg) and 120 pounds (55 kg) for females. Most Great Danes reach physical maturity at approximately three years of age.

Larger dogs are not necessarily better dogs. There is some preliminary evidence that the larger members of the breed might not only be more susceptible to orthopedic disorders, such as elbow dysplasia and hip dysplasia, but also to heart ailments, such as dilated cardiomyopathy. DNA testing is currently being researched and should help answer these and other questions related to size and genetic passage of medical problems.

Great Dane puppies have floppy hound-like ears, unless there is surgical intervention. Be aware that it is not necessary to crop ears in the Great Dane for it to be a purebred. Being a true Great Dane has to do with genetics, not surgery. Most veterinary associations and many breed registries are against altering animals to create an artificial image. Consider carefully your rationale if you decide to have this procedure done.

Hannah has the soft, natural look of a Great Dane whose ears are left uncropped. Hannah is owned by Catherine Woods and Peter Langham.

COAT COLOR, CARE, AND CONDITION *by Jill Evans*

The Great Dane standards of all countries accept five colors for showing: fawn (a rich golden preferred, usually with a black mask), brindle (like fawn with black stripes), black, blue (a deep steel-blue preferred), and harlequin (white with irregular black patches). In Canada, a sixth color, called Boston Black because the markings are like those of the Boston Terrier (in Germany these are called manteltigers or mantle-harlequins, and are shown with blacks), which is really part of the harlequin family, is now accepted at shows. Except for harlequins and Bostons, none should have white on them, although a small patch on the chest or toes is acceptable. All Danes are supposed to have dark brown eyes, although a lighter eye is acceptable in blues and harlequins, which sometimes have two different colored eyes. These colors really belong in three families for breeding purposes: fawns and brindles in one group; blue-bred blacks (try saying that three times quickly!) and blues in another; and harlequins, Bostons, and harl-bred blacks in the third group, which, for breeding purposes only, also includes merles (gray with black spots) and whites. There are also blacks and blues resulting from fawn and black or blue crosses. Indeed these may be very handsome, but should only be used for breeding very judiciously for reasons which may become apparent later. Is this beginning to sound complicated? Well it is, and a little knowledge of basic dominant-recessive genetics is helpful.

In the 1920s and '30s, the German stud books had a section registering Danes that were not the accepted shades and called them "other colors" (Andersfarbige). These registrations prove just how immortal genes are. In spite of half a century of trying to keep colors pure by breeding only within the color-families, look at what showed up: Isabella (a pinkish-brown, probably dilute chocolate or liver), "Drapp" (apparently not the same thing as Isabella), silver-brindle, blue-fawn (only a few years ago one was seen at a show marked like a blue Doberman with tan points), blue-brindle, white and fawn spotted, white with brindle spots, white and brown, gray with brown spots, white with

This Great Dane, owned by Diana Bartlett, is an example of the steel blue coat color.

red spots, blue-white harlequin, and so on (besides the expected merle, which is a necessary part of harlequin breeding but not acceptable at shows). Even in 1971, a chocolate-brindle bitch, out of at least ten generations of pure-color breeding, was shown in California.

Why all these strange colors? How does one avoid them? Ah, that's the whole point. We have

to start thinking of colors in layers that can hide each other. Then we have to pay some attention to patterns and "bleaches," or dilutions. There is a very technical way of explaining all this involving gene loci and alleles, which is covered exhaustively in other books. For the geneticists, suffice it to say that in Danes the following occur: A^s, a^y, rarely at B, b, C, c^{ch},

A brindle coat is a combination of fawn and black in a striped pattern. This brindle Dane is owned by Trish Botterill.

A trio of black Great Dane puppies. The genes for the black coat color can be affected by a dilution factor, which results in a steel blue coat.

rarely c^e and c^a, D, d, E^m, E, e^{br}, possibly e, g, M, m, S, s^i, s^p, s^w, t, and rarely T. Others may occur, but are as yet unknown. We beg the indulgence of the academics in presenting this oversimplified view.

The very top layer is the white of the harlequin, which can be thought of as a blanket with holes in it where other colors can show through. Various things can affect this layer, although they are not very well understood at this point (we'll get back to it later). The next layer is solid black, which can cover up all the other colors. It can also hide a layer that occurs rarely in Danes, but does exist, called brown, liver, or chocolate. These can both be affected by a dilution factor that turns the black color into blue and the chocolate into Isabella, which is an accepted color in Doberman

Pinschers, but seldom seen in Danes, although we know it's there from old stud book accounts. The dilutions, however, are recessive and hidden unless they're present from both parents. The third layer is brindle, which is like fawn with stripes, and it covers up (is dominant to) fawn with a mask, which doesn't cover up anything (it's recessive) and has to be there from both parents for it to show. All this may seem quite straightforward, but we have to remember that the stripes and masks of fawns and brindles can also be affected by the layers above. That is, they're not necessarily black, but can be affected by the dilution factor which would turn them blue, or not be of the black line at all, but chocolate, or even Isabella if the dilution was working there too.

Something that may seem strange at first can also happen. If a blue Dane, which must have the double-recessive dilution present for the color to be evident, is bred to a brindle with a black mask, which is not carrying the recessive dilution factor, the resulting puppies will all be solid black (shudder!). In this case, solid covers up a pattern (brindling and/or mask), but the black of the stripes and mask is dominant to the blue dilution. If the brindle were carrying the blue dilution under the black of its stripes and mask, half the pups would be solid black and the other half solid blue. Imagine what a hodge-podge the next generation could be in these examples! Here come the fawns with blue masks, blues carrying fawn (yes, they can — although both are recessive, remember solid covers pattern), blue-striped brindles, and so on, lurking under those perfectly normal-looking blacks and blues, all ready to show up if one of them were bred to another normal-looking black or blue that was also a carrier. These recessives can be carried unnoticed for endless generations.

Sometimes conscientious breeders of blacks will cross to a fawn or brindle in order to get an improvement in conformation, which is not available in the black family's restricted gene pool. As long as there is no recessive dilution factor (or chocolate, which is also covered up by black) hiding under the solid black coat or the fawn's black mask, this can be perfectly safe, but it is very hard to tell without doing a test breeding, and most people are unwilling to do that. The resulting pups would appear to be normal blacks but would be carriers of the fawn-

brindle recessives, and if they were bred by an unsuspecting buyer to a blue, well, eventually the hodge-podge would show up again. So good breeders will be very careful about who gets any such unneutered pups and will try to make sure that no dilution factors creep into the breeding program.

Harlequin breeding is something else again. There must be a dominant Merle (M) gene and its recessive partner m present for the pattern to show up. Nobody quite understands how this works. Some think there may be a layer under the harlequin white that is the dappled merle

Harlequin breeding is definitely for the experienced breeder. The mating of two beautiful harlequins can produce just about any color variety you can imagine!

color because there are often white Danes with merle patches on them, as well as solid merles. Others think there may be a "clearing" mechanism involved that removes the merling from the white of the harlequin. Others think it's the action of the S or "spotting" gene, which in one of its manifestations produces the Boston pattern of white collar, blaze, stockings, and tail tip; in another a white chest, belly, and legs; and in yet another the small white spots acceptable on all colors, yet undesirable. There are many variations in between.

One thing is sure — two merles must never be bred together because there is a semi-lethal factor connected with the double-dominant *MM*. The offspring are commonly born (if alive) albino, deaf, blind, with tiny eyes, often sterile, and/or constitutionally weak. This applies in other breeds too.

As you can see, harlequin breeding is not for the faint-hearted. Two beautifully marked harls can be bred together and produce nothing but merles and/or mismarked blacks, and if there are other colors in the pedigree, such as fawns, brindles, or blues, there can be "fawniquins,"

"brindiquins," or blues with big white collars and blazes, or, well, use your imagination, anything's possible! Even among harlequin offspring some can be too heavily marked and others too light, or some can have too much merle on them and others too much ticking in the white.

These are the basics of Dane coloration, but there are other facets which need more study, such as the appearance of "sooty" fawns, early graying of masks, and modifiers of all kinds.

Great Dane clubs in most places have rules about breeding the colors only within the families mentioned above, and perhaps the necessity for this has been shown. It's also important to have extended color-marked pedigrees available for this breed, so that mismarks can be avoided.

BEHAVIOR AND PERSONALITY OF THE ACTIVE GREAT DANE
by Nancy E. Holmes

For over 15 years, I did Great Dane rescue, fostering dogs of all colors and backgrounds. I learned a lot about the relationship between the color of a Dane and the likelihood of it turning up in rescue. I also learned to predict which dogs would be the biggest challenge to retrain into well-mannered pets. Based on the color of the Dane, I often knew exactly why a dog was being placed. Here is a synopsis of the things I learned about the colors available and their relationship to Great Dane temperament.

Harlequin Great Danes are white with black patches. This is one of the most difficult colors to breed, and there are several other colors that appear in harlequin litters. Merle color is a gray with black patches, which is a quite common mismark. Merles were often culled from harlequin litters, as the merle color is linked to hereditary defects (such as heart defects) that may prove fatal. Not all merles have these problems, and many make fine pets.

Harlequins with merle patches mixed with the black, or without any solid black patches, are not uncommon. Black Danes with heavy white markings, similar to those of a Boston Terrier, are referred to as Boston Blacks. Solid or nearly solid blacks may also appear in any harlequin litter, as might solid whites and albinos. Occasionally, one will find a color that is considered a total mismark, which is a product of

mix color breeding, such as a fawnequin, which is a white Dane with fawn patches.

The entire harlequin family of colors has other differences besides color that set them apart from the other Danes. In general, the harlequin Dane is busier, noisier, and more aggressive than the other colors. They may be more stubborn about obedience training and more protective of their territory and "rights" as the biggest dog on the block. Harlequins also tend to be the largest of the Danes. They make excellent companion dogs for those ready to follow through with training and exercise and should be considered a dog for the more experienced dog owner. They may easily grow to be too much of a handful for the unprepared novice.

Some black Danes belong to a different family grouping than the Harlequin — that of blacks and blues. Blue Danes are a solid gray ranging from a silver color to a deep slate blue. They are bred back and forth with solid black Danes. Some of the black Danes used in this breeding originally came from harlequin stock, and white toes and white chest patches may be found on some blacks and blues.

In general, blue Danes and blacks out of blue breeding are lighter boned than the Harlequins. They tend to be more shy and are homebodies, happiest with their own families and their own yard. They have the strongest likelihood of becoming fear biters if improperly socialized when young. These Danes benefit from early socialization and gentle training methods, as befits their more sensitive natures. Blue Danes and blacks from blue breeding make excellent companion dogs for those not leading an extensively busy social life, or those who do not expect their dogs to handle constant changes or excessive abuse from small children (no dog should have to handle that, but some do!).

Fawn and brindle Danes belong to the last family. The fawn Dane is the dog most often pictured when one speaks of Great Danes and most fits the stereotype of a big, clumsy, lovable goof as depicted by fiction and cartoons. They vary from a deep red to a pale golden color.

Brindle Danes have a series of small black stripes over a background fawn coat. The amount of striping varies from dogs with light tiger-type stripes to dogs so heavily striped they appear nearly black. All fawns and brindles, when at their best, sport deep black masks and black ears. Mismarks include missing masks, masks that turn blue, and white markings on chest and feet.

Brindles, even though bred back and forth with the mellower fawns, in general may be bouncier than the fawns with slightly higher levels of energy and aggression. Overall, fawns have the repute of having the mellowest temperament, maturing most like the gentle giant often pictured when one speaks of Danes.

All adult Danes have less energy than they did when they were pups. It is a long way from the wild and busy puppy to the adult mature Dane. It usually takes at least three years to get there! A six-month-old Great Dane is the size of the normal large adult dogs of many breeds, yet still has all the puppy urges and needs of its age.

If you don't think you can handle a puppy as large or larger than you are, consider purchasing or adopting an adult dog already past the puppy stages. It's easier to see an adult dog's nature, size, temperament, and activity level than it is to determine exactly how that pup will turn out. If you are a novice, consider starting with an adult dog that you find just perfect, and then add the Dane puppy in later when the adult dog will help you train and exercise it. If there is anything more fun and better company than one Dane, it's two!

When you are picking out a puppy, check the parents' temperament closely. No matter how cute or inexpensive the pups are, do not purchase a puppy from parents that seem overly aggressive or vicious! Even if the owner explains how the dog was 'abused' or had a hard life, risking ownership of a giant dog breed with poor temperament is not worth the gamble of buying one of those pups.

Generalities are not a basis for judging any individual dog. When seeking a Great Dane for a companion or show dog, search diligently to make sure you find the right pup rather than just the right color. A reputable breeder will be able to help you determine which pup is right for you.

Although many Great Danes are happy to sleep the day away in bed or on a sofa, most enjoy having a purpose in their day, making them excellent work dogs. They do not need long daily walks, but they do appreciate events that involve family members. Do not let Great Dane pups run unrestricted because it can increase their risk of developing orthopedic disorders. All Great Danes should attend obedience class, and they need to learn limits to unacceptable behaviors. It is also imperative that *all* Great Danes be obedience trained. A well-loved and well-controlled Great Dane is certain to be a valued family member.

For pet owners, there are several activities to which your Great Dane is well-suited. They not only make great walking and jogging partners, but they are also excellent community volunteers. The breed seems ideally suited to standing still for kisses, hugs, and petting that can last for hours at a time. The loyal and loving Great Dane will be your personal guard dog if properly trained; aggressiveness and viciousness do not fit into the equation.

For Great Dane enthusiasts who want to get into more competitive aspects of the dog world, consider these activities: obedience, showing, guarding, tracking, and Schutzhund.

Overall, when properly bred from sound-bodied parents with steady temperaments and raised and trained with love and firmness, your Great Dane puppy will grow into a dog that warrants being called both the "Apollo of dogs" and the "gentle giant."

SELECTING

**WHAT YOU NEED TO KNOW TO FIND
THE BEST GREAT DANE PUPPY**

Owning the perfect Great Dane rarely happens by accident. On the other hand, owning a "genetic dud" is almost always the result of an impulsive purchase  and failure to do even basic research. Buying this book is a major step in understanding the situation and making intelligent choices.

Facing page: With some research and patience, you can make an informed, intelligent choice when selecting a Great Dane to share your home and life with.

SOURCES

Recently, a large survey was done to determine whether there were more problems seen in animals adopted from pet stores, breeders, private owners, or animal shelters. Somewhat surprisingly, there didn't appear to be any major difference in total number of problems seen from these sources. What was different were the kinds of problems seen in each source. Thus, you can't rely on any one source because there are no standards by which judgments can be made. Most veterinarians will recommend that you select a "good breeder," but there is no way to identify such an individual. A breeder of champion show dogs may also be a breeder of genetic defects.

The best approach is to select a pup from a source that regularly performs genetic screening and has documentation to prove it. If you are intending to be a pet owner, don't worry about whether your pup is show quality. A mark here or there that might disqualify the pup as a show winner has absolutely no impact on its ability to be a loving and healthy pet. Also, the vast majority of dogs will be neutered and not used for breeding anyway. Concentrate on the things that are important.

MEDICAL SCREENING

Whether you are dealing with a breeder, a breed rescue group, a shelter, or a pet store, your approach should be the same. You want to identify a Great Dane that you can live with and screen it for medical and behavioral problems before you make it a permanent family member. If the source you select has not done the important testing needed, make sure they will offer you a health/temperament guarantee before you remove the dog from the premises to have the work done yourself. If this is not acceptable, or they are offering an exchange-only policy, keep moving; this isn't the right place for you to get a dog. As soon as you purchase a Great Dane, pup or adult, go to your veterinarian for a thorough evaluation and testing.

Pedigree analysis is best left to true enthusiasts, but there are some things that you can do even as a novice. Inbreeding is to be discouraged, so check out your four or five generation pedigree and look for names that repeatedly appear. Most breeders linebreed, which is acceptable, so you may see the same *prefix* many times but not the same actual dog or bitch. Reputable breeders will not usually allow inbreeding at least three generations back in the puppy's pedigree. Also, ask the breeder to provide registration numbers on all ancestors in the pedigree for which testing was done through the OFA (Orthopedic Foundation for Animals) and CERF (Canine Eye Registration Foundation). If there are a lot of gaps, the breeder has some explaining to do.

The screening procedure is easier if you select an older dog. Animals can be registered for hips and elbows as young as two years of age by the OFA and by one year of age by Genetic Disease Control (GDC). This is your dog's insurance against hip dysplasia and elbow dysplasia later in life. Great Danes now have a lower incidence of hip dysplasia because of the efforts of conscientious breeders who have been doing the appropriate testing. A verbal testimonial that they've never heard of the condition in their lines is not adequate and probably means they really don't know if they have a problem — move along.

Evaluation is somewhat more complicated in the Great Dane puppy. The PennHip™ procedure can determine risk for developing hip dysplasia in pups as young as 16 weeks of age. For pups younger than that, you should request copies of OFA or GDC registration for both parents. If the parents haven't both been registered, their hip and elbow status should be considered unknown and questionable.

All Great Danes, regardless of age, should be screened for evidence of von Willebrand's disease. This can be accomplished with a simple blood test. The incidence is high enough in the breed that there is no excuse for not performing the test.

For animals older than one year of age, your veterinarian will also want to take a blood sample to check for thyroid function and liver disease in addition to von Willebrand's disease. All are common in the Great Dane. A heartworm test, urinalysis and evaluation of feces for internal parasites is also conducted. If there are any patches of hair loss, a skin scraping should be taken to determine if the dog has evidence of demodectic mange.

Your veterinarian should also perform a very thorough ophthalmologic (eye) examination. The most common eye problems in Great Danes are cataracts, persistent pupillary membranes, and retinal dysplasia. It is best to acquire a pup whose parents have both been screened for heritable eye diseases and certified "clear" by organizations such as CERF. If this has been the case, an examination by your veterinarian is probably sufficient, and referral to an ophthalmologist is only necessary if recommended by your veterinarian.

BEHAVIORAL SCREENING

Medical screening is important, but don't forget temperament. More dogs are killed each year for behavioral reasons than for all medical problems combined. Temperament testing is a valuable, although not infallible, tool in the screening process. The reason that temperament is so important is that many dogs are eventually destroyed because they exhibit undesirable behaviors. Although not all behaviors are evident in young pups (e.g., aggression often takes many months to manifest itself), detecting anxious and fearful pups (and avoiding them) can be very important in the selection process. Traits most identifiable in the young pup include: fear, excitability, low pain threshold, extreme submission, and noise sensitivity.

Pups can be evaluated for temperament as early as seven to eight weeks of age. Some behaviorists, breeders, and trainers recommend objective testing where scores are given in several different categories, others are more casual about the process, since it is only a crude indicator anyway. In general, the evaluation takes place in three stages by someone the pup has not been exposed to. The testing is not done within 72 hours of vaccination or surgery. First, the pup is observed and handled to determine its sociability. Puppies with obvious undesirable traits such as shyness, overactivity, or uncontrollable biting may turn out to be unsuitable. Second, the desired pup is separated from the others and then observed for how it responds when played with and called. Third, the pup is stimulated in various ways and its responses noted. Suitable activities include lying the pup on its side, grooming it, clipping its nails, gently grasping it around the muzzle, and testing its reactions to noise. In a study conducted at the Psychology Department of Colorado State University, they also found that heart rate was a good indicator in this third stage of evaluation. Actually, they noted the resting heart rate, stimulated the pup with a loud noise, and measured how long it took the heart rate to recover to its resting level. Most pups recovered within 36 seconds. Dogs that took considerably longer were more likely to be anxious.

Puppy aptitude tests (PAT) can be given in which a numerical score is given for 11 different traits, with a 1 representing the most assertive or aggressive expression of a trait and a 6 representing disinterest, independence, or inaction. The traits assessed in the PAT include: social attraction to people, following, restraint, social dominance, elevation (lifting off ground by evaluator), retrieving, touch sensitivity, sound sensitivity, prey/chase drive, stability, and energy level. Although the tests do not absolutely predict behaviors, they do tend to do well at predicting puppies at behavioral extremes.

diseases of animals and to establish control programs to lower the incidence of orthopedic diseases in animals. A registry is maintained for both hip dyspлаsia and elbow dysplasia. The ultimate purpose of OFA certification is to provide information to dog owners to assist in the selection of good breeding animals.

What a mixed litter! Make sure you choose a puppy who is healthy and temperamentally sound—don't just pick your favorite color.

ORGANIZATIONS

The Orthopedic Foundation for Animals (OFA) is a nonprofit organization established in 1966 to collect and disseminate information concerning orthopedic

For more information contact your veterinarian or the Orthopedic Foundation for Animals, 2300 Nifong Blvd., Columbia, MO 65201.

The Institute for Genetic Disease Control in Animals (GDC) is a nonprofit organization founded in 1990 which maintains an open registry for orthopedic problems but does not compete with OFA. In an open registry like GDC, owners, breeders, veterinarians, and scientists can trace the genetic history of any particular dog once that dog and close relatives have been registered. At the present time, the GDC operates open registries for hip dysplasia, elbow dysplasia, and osteochondrosis. The GDC is currently developing guidelines for registries of Legg-Calve-Perthes disease, cranio-mandibular osteopathy, and medial patellar luxation. For more information, contact the Institute for Genetic Disease Control in Animals, P.O. Box 222, Davis, CA 95617.

The Canine Eye Registration Foundation (CERF) is an international organization devoted to eliminating hereditary eye diseases from purebred dogs. This organization is similar to OFA that helps eliminate diseases like hip dysplasia. CERF is a nonprofit organization that screens and certifies purebreds as free of heritable eye diseases. Dogs are evaluated by veterinary eye specialists and findings are then submitted to CERF for documentation. The goal is to identify purebreds without heritable eye problems, so they can be used for breeding. Dogs being considered for breeding pro-

Whether you are selecting a puppy or an adult Great Dane, you should always try to find out as much as possible about your new pet's medical and genetic background.

Only dogs that are free of genetic disease should be bred. Through conscientious breeding, we can reduce the possibility of certain diseases in breed lines. Owned by Joan Fonfa.

grams should be screened and certified by CERF on an annual basis, since not all problems are evident in puppies. For more information on CERF, write to CERF, SCC-A, Purdue University, West Lafayette, IN 47907.

Project TEACH™ (Training and Education in Animal Care and Health) is a voluntary accreditation process for those individuals selling animals to the public. It is administered by Pet Health Initiative, Inc. (PHI) and provides instruction on genetic screening as well as many other aspects of proper pet care. TEACH-accredited sources screen animals for a variety of medical, behavioral, and infectious diseases *before* they are sold. Project TEACH™ supports the efforts of registries such as OFA, GDC, and CERF and recommends that all animals sold be registered with the appropriate agencies. For more information on Project TEACH™, send a self-addressed stamped envelope to Pet Health Initiative, P.O. Box 12093, Scottsdale, AZ 85267-2093.

FEEDING & NUTRITION

**WHAT YOU MUST CONSIDER EVERY DAY TO FEED
YOUR GREAT DANE THROUGH HIS LIFETIME**

Nutrition is one of the most important aspects of raising a healthy Great Dane, and yet it is often the source of much controversy between breeders, veterinarians, pet owners, and dog food manufacturers. However, most of these arguments have more to do with marketing than with science.

Facing page: As you can see, Great Danes spend a lot of time growing! They need proper nutrition at all stages of life to attain maximum size and optimum health.

Let's first take a look at dog foods and then determine the needs of our dog. This chapter will concentrate on feeding the pet Great Dane rather than breeding or working Danes.

COMMERCIAL DOG FOODS

Most dog foods are sold based on marketing (i.e., how to make a product appealing to owners while meeting the needs of dogs). Some foods are marketed on the basis of their protein content, others based on a "special" ingredient, and still others are sold because they don't contain certain ingredients (e.g., preserva-

Is it nutritionally sound? Is it reasonably priced? Will my dog like it? These are a few important questions to ask yourself when deciding which commercial dog food to purchase.

tives, soy). We want a dog food that specifically meets our dog's needs, is economical, and causes few if any problems. Most foods come in dry, semi-moist, and canned forms. Some can now be purchased frozen. The "dry" foods are the most economical, containing the least fat and the most preservatives. The canned foods are the most expensive, usually containing the most fat, and the least preservatives (they're 75% water). Semi-moist foods are expensive and high in sugar content, and I do not recommend them for any dogs.

When you're selecting a commercial diet, make sure the food has been assessed by feeding trials for a specific life stage, not just by nutrient analysis. This statement is usually located not far from the ingredient label. In the United States, these trials are performed in accordance with American Association of Feed Control Officials (AAFCO), and in Canada by the Canadian Veterinary Medical Association. This certification is important because it has been found that dog foods currently on the market that provide only a chemical analysis and calculated values but no feeding trial may not provide adequate nutrition. The feeding trials show that the diets meet minimal, not optimal, standards;

however, they are the best tests we currently have.

PUPPY REQUIREMENTS

Soon after pups are born, and certainly within the first 24 hours, they should begin nursing from their mother. This provides them with colostrum, an antibody-rich milk that helps protect them from infection for their first few months of life. Pups should be allowed to nurse for at least six weeks before they are completely weaned from their mother. Supplemental feedings may be started as early as three weeks of age.

By two months of age, pups should be fed puppy food. They are now in an important growth phase. Nutritional deficiencies and/or imbalances during this time of life are more devastating than at any other time. Also, this is not the time to overfeed pups or provide them with "performance" rations. Overfeeding Great Danes can lead to serious skeletal defects such as osteochondrosis, cervical vertebral instability, and hip dysplasia.

Pups should be fed "growth" diets until they are 12–18 months of age. Many Great Danes do not mature until 18 months of age and so benefit from a longer period on these

Nutritional balance is important throughout a dog's life, but it is perhaps most critical in puppyhood, when the crucial growth and development take place.

rations. Pups will initially need to be fed two to three meals daily until they are 12–18 months old, then once to twice daily (preferably twice) when they are converted to adult food. Proper growth diets should be selected based on acceptable feeding trials designed for growing pups. If you can't tell by reading the label, ask your veterinarian for feeding advice.

Remember that pups need "balance" in their diets. Avoid the temptation to supplement with protein, vitamins, or minerals. Calcium supplements have been implicated as a cause of bone and cartilage deformity, especially in large breed puppies. Puppy diets are already heavily fortified with calcium, and supplements tend to unbalance the mineral intake. There is more than adequate proof that these supplements are responsible for many bone deformities seen in these growing dogs.

ADULT DIETS

The goal of feeding adult dogs is one of "maintenance." They have already done all the growing they are going to do and are unlikely to have the digestive problems of elderly dogs. In general, dogs can do well on maintenance rations containing predominantly plant- or animal-based ingredients, as long as that ration has been specifically formulated to meet maintenance level requirements. This contention should be supported by studies performed by the manufacturer in accordance with AAFCO (American Association of Feed Control Officials). In Canada, these products should be certified by the Canadian Veterinary Medical Association to meet maintenance requirements.

There's nothing wrong with feeding a cereal-based diet to dogs on maintenance rations; they are the most economical.

Soy is a common ingredient in cereal-based diets, but may not be completely digested by all dogs, especially Danes. This causes no medical problems, although Danes may tend to be more flatulent on these diets. Similarly, most Great Danes don't tolerate milk products well and tend to be "gassy" when fed dairy products.

When comparing maintenance rations, it must be appreciated that these diets must meet the "minimal" requirements for confined dogs, not necessarily optimal levels. Most dogs will benefit when fed diets that contain easily digested ingredients that provide nutrients at least slightly above minimal requirements. Typically, these foods will be intermediate in price between the most expensive super-premium diets and the cheapest generic diets. Select only those diets that have been substantiated by feeding trials to meet maintenance requirements, those that contain wholesome ingredients, and those recommended by your veterinarian. Don't select based on price alone, on company advertising, or on total protein content.

GERIATRIC DIETS

Great Danes are considered elderly when they are about five

years of age. There are certain changes that occur as dogs age that alter their nutritional requirements. As pets age, their metabolism slows, and this must be accounted for. If maintenance rations are fed in the same amounts while metabolism is slowing, weight gain may result. Obesity is the last thing one wants to contend with in an elderly pet since it increases their risk of several other health-related problems. As pets age, most of their organs do not function as well as in youth. The digestive system, the liver, pancreas, and gallbladder are not functioning at peak effect. The intestines have more difficulty extracting all the nutrients from the food consumed. A gradual decline in kidney function is considered a normal part of aging.

A responsible approach to geriatric nutrition is to realize that degenerative changes are a normal part of aging. Our goal is to minimize the potential damage done by taking this into account while the dog is still well. If we wait until an elderly dog is ill before we change the diet, we have a much harder job.

Elderly dogs need to be treated as individuals. While some benefit from the nutrition found in "senior" diets, others might do better on the highly-digestible puppy and super-premium diets. These latter diets provide an excellent blend of digestibility and amino acid content; but, unfortunately, many are higher in salt and phosphorus than the older pet really needs.

An active dog should have no trouble staying in shape and will do well on a maintenance diet. However, an older dog who is less active and has a slower metabolism will have different nutritional needs.

Older dogs are also more prone to developing arthritis, and therefore, it is important not to overfeed them since obesity puts added stress on the joints. For animals with joint pain, supplementing the diet with fatty acid combinations containing cis-linoleic acid, gamma-linolenic acid, and eicosapentaenoic acid can be quite beneficial.

MEDICAL CONDITIONS AND DIET

It is important to keep in mind that dietary choices can affect the development of orthopedic diseases such as hip dysplasia, cervical vertebral instability, and osteochondrosis. When feeding a pup at risk, avoid high-calorie diets and try to feed several times a day rather than ad libitum. Sudden growth spurts are to be avoided because they result in joint instability. Recent research has also suggested that the electrolyte balance of the diet may also play a role in the development of hip dysplasia. Rations that had more balance between the positively and negatively charged elements in the diet (e.g., sodium, potassium, chloride) were less likely to promote hip dysplasia in susceptible dogs. Also, avoid supplements of calcium, phosphorus, and vitamin D as they can interfere with normal bone and cartilage development. The fact is that calcium levels in the body are carefully regulated by hormones (such as calcitonin and parathormone) as well as vitamin D. Supplementation disturbs this normal regulation and can cause many problems. It has also been shown that calcium supplementation can interfere with the proper absorption of zinc from the intestines. If you really feel the need to supplement your dog, select products such as eicosapentaenoic/gamma-linolenic fatty acid combinations or small amounts of vitamin C.

You can't prevent heart disease in dogs entirely by dietary changes, but there are some things that you can do to help. In addition to selecting properly formulated diets, nutritional supplements can be useful additions in this case. Some breeds prone to dilated cardiomyopathy have been shown to respond to supplements of L-carnitine, taurine, and/or coenzyme Q. Although Great Danes are commonly afflicted with this disorder, a nutritional link has not been determined in this breed. Until the research has been done, it may be advisable to begin supplementation with coenzyme Q_{10} by two years of age. A dose has not been precisely determined for dogs, but some cardiologists are using doses of 30—90 mg/day. The soft gelatin capsules are preferred and can be orally administered or punctured and squirted onto the food. This has been shown to improve heart muscle function and may delay the onset of clinical heart disease in susceptible animals.

Diet can't prevent bloat (gastric dilatation/volvulus), but changing feeding habits can make a difference. Initially, the bloat occurs when the stomach becomes distended with swallowed air. This air is swallowed as a consequence of gulping food or water, stress and exercising too close to mealtime. This is where we can make a difference. Divide meals and feed your pet three times daily rather than all at once. Soak dry dog food in water before feeding to decrease the tendency to gulp the food. If you want to feed dry food only, add some large clean chew toys to the feed bowl so that the dog has to "pick" to get at the food and can't gulp it. Putting the food bowl on a step-stool, so the dog doesn't have to stretch to get the food, may also be helpful. Finally, don't allow any exercise for at least one hour before and after feeding.

Fat supplements are probably the most common supplements purchased from pet supply stores. They frequently promise to add luster, gloss, and sheen to the coat, and consequently, make dogs look healthy. The only fatty acid that is essential for this purpose is cis-linoleic acid, which is found in flaxseed oil, sunflower seed oil, and safflower oil. Corn oil is a suitable, but less effective alternative. Most of the other oils found in retail supplements are high in saturated and monounsaturated fats and are not beneficial for shiny fur or healthy skin. For dogs with allergies, arthritis, high blood pressure (hypertension), high cholesterol, and some heart ailments, other fatty acids may be prescribed by a veterinarian. The important ingredients in these products are gamma-linolenic acid (GLA), eicosapentaenoic acid (EPA), and docosahexaenoic acid (DHA). These products have gentle and natural anti-inflammatory properties. Don't be fooled by imitations. Most retail fatty acid supplements do not contain these functional forms of the essential fatty acids — look for gamma-linolenic acid, eicosapentaenoic acid, and docosahexaenoic acid on the label.

HEALTH

**PREVENTIVE MEDICINE AND HEALTH CARE
FOR YOUR GREAT DANE**

Keeping your Great Dane healthy requires preventive health care. This is not only the most effective but the least expensive way to battle illness. Good preventive care starts even before puppies are born. The dam should be well cared for, vaccinated, and free of infections and parasites.

Facing page: A Great Dane puppy cannot become a strong, healthy adult without consistent preventive health care and maintenance.

Hopefully, both parents were screened for important genetic diseases (e.g., von Willebrands's disease), were registered with the appropriate agencies (e.g., OFA, GDC, CERF), showed no evidence of medical or behavioral problems, and were found to be good candidates for breeding.

This gives the pup a good start in life. If all has been planned well, the dam will pass on resistance to disease to her pups that will last for the first few months of life. However, the dam can also pass on parasites, infections, genetic diseases, and more.

TWO TO THREE WEEKS OF AGE

By two to three weeks of life, it is usually necessary to start pups on a regimen to control worms. Although dogs benefit from this parasite control, the primary reason for doing this is human health. After whelping, the dam often sheds large numbers of worms, even if she tested negative previously. This is because many worms lay dormant in tissues, and the stress of delivery causes parasite release into the environment. Because studies have shown that 75% do, assume that all puppies potentially have worms. Thus, we in-

Healthy parents should produce healthy puppies. Dane pups start out with an advantage in life if they come from a sire and dam who have been properly vaccinated, screened for genetic and behavioral problems, and are parasite-free.

stitute worm control early to protect the people in the house from worms more than the pups themselves. The deworming is repeated every two to three weeks until your veterinarian feels the condition is under control. Nursing bitches should be treated at the same time because they often shed worms during this time. Only use products recommended by your veterinarian. Over-the-counter parasiticides have been responsible for deaths in pups.

SIX TO TWENTY WEEKS OF AGE

Most puppies are weaned from their mother at six to eight weeks of age. Weaning shouldn't be done too early so that pups have the opportunity to socialize with their littermates and dam. This is important for them to be able to respond to other dogs later in life. There is no reason to rush the weaning process unless the dam can't produce enough milk to feed the pups.

Pups are usually first examined by their veterinarian at six to eight weeks of age which is when most vaccination schedules commence. If pups are exposed to many other dogs at this young age, veterinarians often opt for vaccinating with

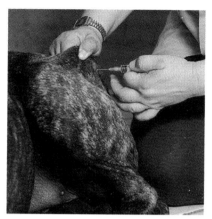

Your Great Dane should begin receiving vaccinations between six and eight weeks of age. Certain vaccinations are necessary before the puppy can be socialized, and some will require annual boosters.

inactivated parvovirus at six weeks of age. When exposure isn't a factor, most veterinarians would rather wait to see the pup at eight weeks of age. At this point, they can also do a preliminary dental evaluation to see that all the puppy teeth are coming in correctly, check to see that the testicles are properly descending in males and that there are no health reasons to prohibit vaccination at this time. Heart murmurs, wandering knee-caps (luxating patellae), juvenile cataracts, persistent hyperplastic primary vitreous (a congenital eye disease), and hernias are usually evident by this time.

Your veterinarian may also be able to perform temperament testing on the pup by eight weeks of age or recommend someone to do it for you. Although temperament testing is not completely accurate, it can often predict which pups are most anxious and fearful. Some form of temperament evaluation is important because behavioral problems account for more animals being euthanized (killed) each year than all medical conditions combined.

Recently, some veterinary hospitals have been recommending neutering pups as early as six to eight weeks of age. A study done at the University of Florida College of Veterinary Medicine over a span of more than four years concluded there was no increase in complications when animals were neutered when less than six months of age. The evaluators also concluded that the surgery appeared to be less stressful when done in young pups.

Most vaccination schedules consist of injections being given at 6–8, 10–12, and 14–16 weeks of age. Ideally, vaccines should not be given closer than two weeks apart and three to four weeks seems to be optimal. Each vaccine usually consists of several different viruses (e.g., parvovirus, distemper, parainfluenza, hepatitis) combined into one injection. Coronavirus can be given as a separate vaccination according to this same schedule if pups are at risk. Some veterinarians and breeders advise another parvovirus booster at 18–20 weeks of age. A booster is given for all vaccines at one year of age and annually thereafter. For animals at increased risk of exposure, parvovirus vaccination may be given as often as four times a year. A new vaccine for canine cough (tracheobronchitis) is squirted into the nostrils. It can be given as early as six weeks of age, if pups are at risk. Leptospirosis vaccination is given in some geographic areas and likely offers protection for six to eight months. The initial series consists of three to four injections spaced two to three weeks apart, starting as early as ten weeks of age. Rabies vaccine is given as a separate injection at three months of age, then repeated when the pup is one year old, then every one to three years depending on local risk and government regulation.

Between 8 and 14 weeks of age, use every opportunity to expose the pup to as many people and situations as possible. This is part of the critical socialization period that will determine how good a pet your dog will become. This is not the time to abandon a puppy for eight hours while you go to work. This is also not the time to punish your dog in any way, shape, or form.

This is the time to introduce your dog to neighborhood cats, birds, and other creatures. Hold off on exposure to other dogs until after the second vaccination in the series. You don't want your new friend to pick up contagious diseases from dogs it meets in its travels before it has adequate protection. By 12 weeks of age, your pup should be ready for social outings with other dogs. Do it! It's a great way for your dog to feel comfortable around members of its own species. Walk the streets and introduce your pup to everybody you meet. Your

goal should be to introduce your dog to every type of person or situation it is likely to encounter in its life. Take it in cars, elevators, buses, subways; to parade grounds and beaches; you want it to habituate to all environments. Expose your pup to kids,

Pets, pets, and more pets! It is important that all of your family pets get along with each other—Janet DeMaria's Great Danes treat her three cats as their "pets."

teenagers, old people, people in wheelchairs, people on bicycles, people in uniforms. The more varied the exposure, the better the socialization.

Proper identification of your pet is also important, since it minimizes the risk of theft and increases the chances that your pet will be returned to you if it is lost. There are several different options. Microchip implantation is a relatively painless procedure involving the subcutaneous injection of an implant the size of a grain of rice. This implant does not act as a beacon if your pet is missing. However, if your pet turns up at a veterinary clinic or shelter and is checked with a scanner, the chip provides information about you that can be used to quickly reunite you with your pet. This method of identification is reasonably priced, permanent in nature, and performed at most veterinary clinics. Another option is tattooing, which can be done on the inner ear or on the skin of the abdomen. Most purebreds are given a number by the associated registry (e.g., American Kennel Club, The Kennel Club, United Kennel Club, Canadian Kennel Club, etc.) that is used for identification. Alternatively, permanent numbers such as social security numbers (telephone numbers and addresses may change during the life of your pet) can be used in the tattooing process. There are several different tattoo registries maintaining lists of dogs, their tattoo codes, and their owners. Finally, identifying collars and tags provide quick information but can be separated from your pet if it is lost or stolen. They work best when combined with a permanent identification system such as microchip implantation or tattooing.

FOUR TO SIX MONTHS OF AGE

At 16 weeks of age, when your pup gets the last in its series of regular induction vaccinations, ask your veterinarian about evaluating the pup for hip dysplasia with the PennHip™ technique. This helps predict the risk of developing hip dysplasia as well as degenerative joint disease. Great Dane breeders have done an excellent job decreasing the incidence of hip dysplasia through routine screening and registration programs. Since anesthesia is typically required for the procedure, many veterinarians like to do the evaluation at the same time as neutering.

At this time, it is very worthwhile to perform a diagnostic test for von Willebrand's disease, an inherited disorder that causes uncontrolled bleeding. A simple blood test is all that is required, but it may need to be sent to a special laboratory to have the test performed. You will be extremely happy you had the foresight to have this done before neutering. If your dog does have a bleeding problem, it will be necessary to take special precautions during surgery. This is also a great time to run the parvovirus antibody titer to determine how well your dog has responded to the vaccination series.

SIX TO TWELVE MONTHS OF AGE

As a general rule, neuter your animal at about six months of age unless you fully intend to breed it. As we know, neutering can be safely done at eight weeks of age but this is still not a common practice. Neutering not only stops the possibility of pregnancy and undesirable behaviors but can prevent several health problems as well. It is a well-established fact that pups spayed before their first heat have a dramatically reduced incidence of mammary (breast) cancer. Likewise, neutered males significantly decrease their incidence of prostate disorders.

When your pet is six months of age, your veterinarian will want to take a blood sample to perform a heartworm test. If the test is negative and shows no evidence of heartworm infection, the pup will go on heartworm prevention therapy. Some veterinarians are even recommending preventive therapy in younger pups. This might be a

Taking your dog around the neighborhood is a good way to familiarize people with your dog. If your dog is lost, it will help if people recognize him—and who could forget the face of this harlequin Dane? Owned by the Lemmons family.

once-a-day regimen, but newer therapies can be given on a once-a-month basis. As a bonus, most of these heartworm preventatives also help prevent internal parasites.

If your Great Dane has any patches of hair loss, your veterinarian will want to perform a skin scraping with a scalpel blade to see if any demodex mites are responsible. If there is a problem, don't lose hope; about 90% of demodicosis cases can be

Nylabone® products keep these Great Danes busy while promoting their dental health. The raised dental tips on the Plaque Attackers® and the Hercules™ bone help to clean the dogs' teeth as they chew.

each week and perhaps using dental rinses. It is a sad fact that 85% of dogs over four years of age have periodontal disease and "doggy breath." In fact, it is so common that most people think it is "normal." Well, it is normal — as normal as bad breath would be in people if they never brushed their teeth. Brush your dog's teeth regularly with a special toothbrush and toothpaste, and you can greatly reduce the incidence of tartar buildup, bad breath, and gum disease. Provide the Puppy Bone™ from Nylabone® and Gumabone® to puppies as early as eight to ten weeks. Nylabones® not only help in the proper development of the puppy's jaw and the emergence of adult teeth but help to keep the teeth clean . . . and the breath fresh. Better preventive care means that dogs live a long time, and they'll enjoy their sunset years more if they still have their teeth. Ask

cured with supportive care only. However, it's important to diagnose it early before scarring results.

Another part of the six-month visit should be a thorough dental evaluation to make sure all the permanent teeth have correctly erupted. If they haven't, this will be the time to correct the problem. Correction should only be performed to make the animal more comfortable and promote normal chewing. The procedures should never be used to cosmetically improve the appearance of a dog used for show purposes or breeding.

After the dental evaluation, you should start implementing home dental care. In most cases, this will consist of brushing the teeth one or more times your veterinarian for details on home dental care.

THE FIRST SEVEN YEARS

At one year of age, your dog should be examined again and have boosters for all vaccines. Your veterinarian will also want to do a very thorough physical examination to look for early evidence of problems. This might include taking radiographs (x-rays) of the hips and elbows to look for evidence of dysplastic changes. Genetic Disease Control (GDC) will certify hips and elbows at 12 months of age; Orthopedic Foundation for Animals won't issue certification until 24 months of age.

At 12 months of age, it's also a great time to have some blood samples analyzed to provide background information. Although few Great Danes experience clinical problems at this young age, troubles may be starting. Therefore, it is a good idea to have baseline levels of thyroid hormones (free and total), TSH, blood cell counts, organ chemistries, and cholesterol levels. This can serve as a valuable comparison to samples collected in the future.

Each year, preferably around the time of your pet's birthday, it's time for another veterinary visit. This visit is a wonderful

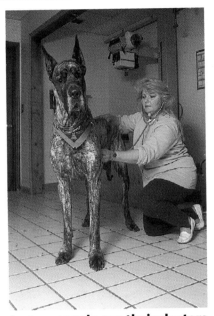

Just as people see their doctors for yearly physicals, dogs need annual check ups to maintain good health and prevent potential problems. Owned by Dennis G. Rugg.

opportunity for a thorough clinical examination rather than just "shots." Since 85% of dogs have periodontal disease by four years of age, veterinary intervention does not seem to be as widespread as it should be. The examination should include visually inspecting the ears, eyes (a great time to start scrutinizing for progressive retinal atrophy, cataracts, etc.), mouth (don't wait for gum disease), and groin; listening (auscultation) to the lungs and heart; feeling (palpating) the lymph nodes and abdomen; and answering all of your questions about optimal health care. In addition, booster vaccinations are given during these times, feces are checked for parasites, urine is analyzed, and blood samples may be collected for analysis. One of the tests run on the blood sample is for heartworm antigen. In areas of the country where heartworm is only present in the spring, summer, and fall (it's spread by mosquitoes), blood samples are collected and evaluated about a month prior to the mosquito season. Other routine blood tests are for blood cells (hematology), organ chemistries, thyroid levels, and electrolytes.

By two years of age, most veterinarians prefer to begin preventive dental cleanings, often referred to as "prophies." Anesthesia is required, and the veterinarian or veterinary dentist will use an ultrasonic scaler to remove plaque and tartar from above and below the gum line, then polish the teeth so that plaque has a harder time sticking to the teeth. Radiographs (x-rays) and fluoride treatments are other options. It is now known that it is plaque, not tartar, that initiates inflammation in the gums. Since scaling and root planing remove more tar-

tar than plaque, veterinary dentists have begun using a new technique called PerioBUD (periodontal bactericidal ultrasonic debridement). The ultrasonic treatment is quicker, disrupts more bacteria, and is less irritating to the gums. With tooth polishing to finish up the procedure, gum healing is better, and owners can start home care sooner. Each dog has its own dental needs that must be addressed, but most veterinary dentists recommend prophies annually. Be sure too that your Great Dane always has a Nylabone® available to do his part in keeping his teeth clean.

At four to five years of age, your veterinarian will probably want to start screening for dilated cardiomyopathy, since this is so common in Great Danes. Chest radiographs (x-rays) aren't usually too helpful; ultrasound examinations (echocardiography) and electrocardiograms (EKGs) are the preferred tests. Annual tests are usually sufficient, and it is extremely important to diagnose the condition early because it is such a devastating and life-threatening disease.

SENIOR GREAT DANES

Great Danes are considered seniors when they reach about

seven years of age. Veterinarians still usually only need to examine them once a year, but it is now important to start screening for geriatric problems. Accordingly, blood profiles, urinalysis, chest radiographs (x-rays), and electrocardiograms (EKG) are recommended on an annual basis. When problems are caught early, they are much more likely to be successfully managed. This is as true in canine medicine as it is in human medicine.

Good health and vitality are evident in a well-maintained dog— notice Spock's bright, clear eyes and shiny coat. Owned by Robert Lavin.

MEDICAL PROBLEMS

RECOGNIZED GENETIC CONDITIONS SPECIFICALLY RELATED TO THE GREAT DANE

Many conditions appear to be especially prominent in Great Danes. Sometimes it is possible to identify the genetic basis of a  problem, but in many cases, we must be satisfied with merely identifying the breeds that are a risk and how the conditions can be identified, treated, and prevented.

Facing page: As a responsible Great Dane owner, you should have a basic understanding of the medical problems that specifically affect the breed.

Following are some conditions that have been recognized as being common in the Great Dane, but this listing is certainly not complete. Also, many genetic conditions may be common in certain breed lines, not in the breed in general.

ACNE

Acne is not simply a bacterial infection. Certain breeds, such as the Great Dane, are particularly at risk. Like the situation in people, waxy deposits clog up the hair follicles (pores), especially in the chin area. Most affected dogs, not surprisingly, start to have problems during puberty, and there is usually some reprieve by about three years of age.

Acne does not respond well to antibiotics, and these are not needed for successful treatment. Gentle cleansing pads that are sold for use in people can help clear debris from the clogged pores. Warm poultices can help bring the pus accumulation to a "head." In some recalcitrant cases, topical benzoyl peroxide scrubs and gels are helpful; vitamin A-derived retinoid creams can also be helpful. Because this is a cosmetic disorder and doesn't affect the health of the animal, treatment should not be overdone.

ACRAL LICK DERMATITIS

Few things are as frustrating to veterinarians as dealing with acral lick dermatitis, or lick granuloma, a problem caused by dogs licking incessantly at a spot on their leg. Dogs start licking at a spot, and before you know it, they have removed layers of skin leaving a raw open area. The reason for this is unknown, but many theories have come and gone, and we're still not positive why a dog would do this kind of damage to itself.

Great Danes are, in most studies, one of the most common breeds affected with this disorder, and males are affected twice as often as females. Some recent research has even shown that there may be some nerve deficits in dogs that develop this condition. Other research has suggested that boredom may be a precipitating cause that eventuates in a compulsive behavior.

It is important to diagnose these cases carefully, since some cases may actually be a result of another disease condition, which will need to be addressed. Therefore, often biopsies, microbial cultures, and even radiographs (x-rays) are needed to help confirm a diagnosis.

Treatment is often frustrating because it is difficult to predict the chances of success without knowing the cause. Most therapies use anti-inflammatory agents, but a variety of other options exist, including tranquilizers, female sex hormones, anti-anxiety drugs, and medications that reverse the effects of narcotics. More exotic treatments, such as injecting cobra antivenin into the site, radiation therapy, and cryosurgery, have been used in the past but often have limited success. The newest craze is to use anti-anxiety drugs and antidepressants to treat the "compulsive" aspect of the disorder.

Prevention is difficult because the ultimate cause of the problem has not been determined. Until we know more, our advice must be that affected dogs, their parents, and their siblings should not be used in breeding programs.

CERVICAL VERTEBRAL INSTABILITY

CVI, or wobbler syndrome, is caused by an instability in the intervertebral disks in the neck area, and once again, Great Danes are one of the main breeds affected. When the disk destabilizes and puts pressure on the spinal cord, the result is severe neck pain. Affected Great Danes start with problems between 3–18 months of age, while Doberman Pinschers (another breed prone to the condition) usually develop clinical signs later, be-

We can all relate to how 11-month-old Spock is feeling—he's in that awkward stage of adolescence, pimples and all!

tween four to ten years of age. Affected dogs develop clinical signs (symptoms) associated with a narrowing of the spinal canal and compression of the spinal cord. Preliminary research suggests that excess dietary calcium, genetic factors, and overfeeding may all be involved.

The diagnosis is confirmed by taking radiographs (x-rays), and special dyes are often used to help outline the defect. Strict rest and anti-inflammatory therapy (usually with corticosteroids) are used initially to quickly reduce the amount of inflammation in the spinal canal. This conservative therapy will often improve the clinical signs (symptoms) but cannot be expected to correct the underlying spinal defect. Some dogs can be maintained on long-term cortisone therapy with adequate control, but most others eventually develop progressive problems. If permanent damage is not evident, surgical decompression and stabilization is the treatment of choice.

The best way to prevent wobbler syndrome in your Great Dane is to avoid calcium supplementation, feed several small meals daily (rather than one large meal or ad libitum feedings), and not purchase a pup with a family history of vertebral instability.

COLOR DILUTION ALOPECIA

Color dilution alopecia, also known as color mutant alopecia, refers to the patchy poor haircoat that develops in animals bred for abnormally-colored hair, the "blue" Great Dane. The colors may be interesting, but the hair follicles that produce them eventually become "dysplastic," and a variety of skin and fur problems result in virtually every blue Great Dane. The coat is normal in pups, but eventually the abnormally-colored hairs fall out and the skin becomes dry and scaly.

If there is any question about the cause of the problem, some of the abnormally-colored hairs can be plucked and observed under a microscope, or a skin biopsy can be taken and evaluated by a pathologist. There is no way to cure these dogs, and treatment is therefore lifelong and includes use of medicated shampoos and moisturizers. It is best not to own a "blue," and certainly a mistake to breed one, unless you are a real enthusiast. These dogs require more care than the average owner is willing to provide.

Prevention is easy, since there is no reason for the average pet owner to buy one of these color-diluted Danes —stick with other varieties. Prevention requires selecting breeding stock from animals that are normal in color and have never produced diluted pups. Dogs that have produced any diluted pups must be considered carriers for the trait.

DEAFNESS

Deafness refers to a loss of hearing, which can be complete or partial. The condition is associated with merle coloration and therefore, is an important concern in the Great Dane. To a lesser extent, it is also seen in harlequin Danes. Because the incidence of deafness is high in merle Great Danes and because deaf dogs don't usually make good pets (and definitely shouldn't be used for breeding), it is recommended that all breeding merle Great Danes have their hearing tested. Pups should be tested when weaned at six to eight weeks of age and before they are sold. Whereas dogs that are deaf in one ear can still make good pets, they should be neutered so as not to contribute genetically to future generations. Dogs that are deaf in both ears make poor pets because they are difficult to teach and are easily startled.

You can tell subjectively if a dog can hear by shaking your keys, clapping your hands or otherwise trying to attract its attention while out of sight. However, the definitive way to test is known as BAER (brainstem auditory-evoked response) testing, which is completely painless and can detect any loss of hearing in one or both ears. This testing is available from veterinary schools and referral centers. Ideally, every merle Great Dane should be BAER tested before breeding, and all merle pups should be BAER tested before being sold.

DEMODICOSIS

Demodex mites are present on the skin of all dogs, but in some animals born with a defective immune system the numbers increase and begin to cause problems. Great Danes are usually cited as one of the most common breeds affected with this condition. Although it is thought to be genetically transmitted, the mode of transmission has never been conclusively demonstrated.

Most cases of demodicosis are seen in young pups, and fully 90% of cases self-cure with little or no medical intervention by the time these dogs reach immunologic maturity at 18—36 months of age. In these cases, it is suspected that the immune system is marginally compromised and eventually matures and gets the condition under control. On the other hand, some pups (about 10% of those initially affected) do not get better and, in fact, become progressively worse. These are thought to have more severe immunologic compromise and are often labeled as having "generalized demodicosis."

The diagnosis is easily made by scraping the skin with a scalpel blade and looking at the collected debris under a microscope. The demodex mites are cigar-shaped and are easily seen. What is harder to identify is the immunologic defect that allowed the condition to occur in the first place. Recent research has suggested the problem may be linked to a decrease in interleukin-2 response, but the genetics is still a question.

If the cause of the immune dysfunction can be cured, the mange will resolve on its own. Likewise, if the pup outgrows its immunologic immaturity or defect, the condition will self-cure. This process can best be assisted by ensuring a healthy diet, treating for any internal parasites or other diseases, and perhaps using cleansing shampoos and nutritional supplements that

help bolster the immune system. However, if the condition does not resolve on its own, or if it is getting worse despite conservative therapy, special mite-killing treatments are necessary. Amitraz is the most common dip used, but experimentally, milbemycin oxime and ivermectin given daily have shown some promising results. It must be remembered that killing the mites will not restore the immune system to normal.

Regarding prevention, it is best not to breed dogs with a history of demodicosis, and dogs with generalized demodicosis should *never* be bred. Although the genetic nature of this disease has not been decisively proven, it doesn't make sense to add affected individuals to the gene pool of future generations.

DILATED CARDIOMYOPATHY

Dilated cardiomyopathy refers to a defect in which the heart muscle becomes thin and stretched, much like a balloon. In that condition, it is not a very effective pump, and eventually, affected dogs die from heart failure. Great Danes are one of the most commonly affected breeds, so it is a very important medical concern in this breed.

Although a genetic tendency is suspected, long-term studies

are not yet available. In some breeds, a nutritional mechanism has been proposed that this might involve L-carnitine, taurine, and/or coenzyme Q. In Boxers, there appears to be an autosomal genetic association, likely dominant in nature. Recent studies in the American Cocker Spaniel seem to suggest that taurine (another amino acid) may be implicated, as it is in the feline form of the disease. However, it is impossible to extrapolate research from one breed to another. Until the research is done in Great Danes, we will just have to wait to draw conclusions. As if this isn't confusing enough, some researchers suspect that viruses might also be involved, since there is some human research indicating that this might be the case in people.

Early in the course of the disease, affected animals seem normal. It is only when they show signs of heart failure that most owners seek veterinary attention. Early signs might include depression, coughing, exercise intolerance, weakness, respiratory distress, decreased appetite, and even fainting. In some breeds, and especially in the Great Dane, sudden death may be the first clue that something was ever wrong. Thus, routine thorough veterinary examinations are very important, especially in the young and middle-aged adult. Characteristic murmurs may be heard in some cases, and there is often an enlarged heart field evident with careful auscultation (listening with a stethoscope).

The symptoms of dilated cardiomyopathy are often hard to notice in a breed like the Great Dane, since many affected animals will appear healthy in the early stages of the disease.

In some cases the heart rate is increased, which might indicate atrial fibrillation, a common sequel to cardiomyopathy. However, in most cases, radiographs (x-rays), electrocardiograms (EKGs), and echocardiograms (ultrasound examinations) are required for definitive diagnosis. In most breeds, x-rays reveal an enlarged heart, but the Great Dane seems to be an exception in that heart size doesn't usually increase until late in the course of the disease. Echocardiograms are painless studies using ultrasound examination that are extremely useful in making the diagnosis. Electrocardiograms (EKGs) also have their place. Recent studies have shown that most dogs (especially Great Danes) with early cardiomyopathy have ventricular premature contractions (VPCs), which are indicators of increased risk to developing actual cardiomyopathy. These VPCs may not be evident all the time when EKGs are taken, so 24-hour studies with a Holter monitor are sometimes necessary, as they are in people.

There is no cure for cardiomyopathy, but some breeds respond well to megadoses of specific nutrients. However, there has been no specific association with nutritional irregularities in the Great Dane. Since these nutrients are quite safe, some individuals supplement with L-carnitine, taurine, and coenzyme Q even though they haven't been proven to be beneficial in the Great Dane.

Digoxin (a digitalis derivative) is often used to treat the condition, as are beta-1 blockers and vasodilators. Milrinone, an experimental drug, has been very effective in dogs with heart muscle failure but is not yet available for dogs or people. All dogs with cardiomyopathy that are treated with drugs only eventually succumb to the disease.

Right now there are no foolproof ways to prevent cardiomyopathy. The best choice is to avoid pups that have a family history of cardiomyopathy. In many cases, it will be necessary to know medical history back at least three generations.

ELBOW DYSPLASIA

Elbow dysplasia refers to an entire complex of disorders that affect the elbow joint. Several different processes might be involved including ununited anconeal process, fragmented medial coronoid process, osteochondritis of the medial humeral condyle, or incomplete ossification of the humeral condyle. Elbow dysplasia and osteochondrosis are disorders of young dogs, with problems usually starting between four and seven months of age. The usual manifestation is a sudden onset of lameness. In time, the continued inflammation results in arthritis in those affected joints.

Although Great Danes are often listed as being particularly prone to elbow dysplasia, the research says otherwise. However, since the incidence is so low, continued registration is recommended because it should be possible to completely eliminate the condition in Great Danes by conscientious breeding.

Radiographs (x-rays) are taken of the elbow joints and submitted to a registry for evaluation. The Orthopedic Foundation for Animals (OFA) will assign a breed registry number to those animals with normal elbows that are over 24 months of age. Abnormal elbows are reported as grade I to III, where grade III elbows have well-developed degenerative joint disease (arthritis). Normal elbows on individuals 24 months or older are assigned a breed registry number and are periodically reported to parent breed clubs. Genetic Disease Control for Animals (GDC) maintains an open registry for elbow dysplasia and assigns a registry number to those individuals with normal elbows at 12 months of age or older. Only animals with normal elbows should be used for breeding.

There is strong evidence to support the contention that OCD of the elbow is an inherited disease, likely controlled by many genes. Preliminary research (in Labrador Retrievers) also suggests that the different forms of elbow dysplasia are inherited independently. Therefore, breeding stock should be selected from those animals without a history of osteochondrosis, preferably for several generations. Unaffected dogs producing offspring with OCD, FCP (fragmented coronoid process), or both should not be bred again, and unaffected first-degree relatives (e.g., siblings) should not be used for breeding either.

Other than genetics, the most likely associations made to date

Walking your dog provides him with controlled, supervised exercise that will not put him at risk of injury (and it's good for you, too).

suggest that feeding diets high in calories, calcium, and protein promote the development of osteochondrosis in susceptible dogs. Also, animals that are allowed to exercise in an unregulated fashion are at increased risk, since they are more likely to sustain cartilage injuries.

The management of dogs with OCD is a matter of much debate and controversy. Some recommend surgery to remove the damaged cartilage before permanent damage is done. Others recommend conservative therapy of rest and pain-killers. The most common drugs used are aspirin and polysulfated glycosaminoglycans. Most veterinarians agree that the use of cortisone-like compounds (corticosteroids) creates more problems than it treats in this condition. What seems clear is that some dogs will respond to conservative therapies, while others need surgery. Surgery is often helpful if performed before there is significant joint damage.

GASTRIC DILATATION/ VOLVULUS

Gastric dilatation, or bloat, occurs when the stomach becomes distended with air. The air gets swallowed into the stomach when susceptible dogs exercise, gulp their food/water, or are stressed. Although bloat can occur at any age, it becomes more common as susceptible dogs get older. Purebreds are three times more likely to suffer from bloat than mutts, and in most studies, Great Danes are the most common breed affected.

Bloat on its own is uncomfortable, but it is the possible consequences that make it life-threatening. As the stomach fills with air, like a balloon, it can twist on itself and impede the flow of food within the stomach as well as the blood supply to the stomach and other digestive organs. This twisting (volvulus or torsion) not only makes the bloat worse, but also results in toxins being released into the bloodstream and death of blood-deprived tissues. These events, if allowed to progress, will usually result in death within four to six hours. Approximately one-third of dogs with bloat and volvulus will die, even under appropriate hospital care.

Affected dogs will be uncomfortable, restless, depressed, and have extended abdomens. They need veterinary attention immediately, or they will suffer from shock and die! There are a variety of surgical procedures to correct the abnormal positioning of the stomach and organs. Intensive medical therapy is also necessary to treat for shock, acidosis, and the effects of toxins.

Bloat can't be completely prevented, but there are some easy things to do to greatly reduce the risk. Don't leave food down for dogs to eat as they wish. Divide the day's meals into three portions and feed morning, afternoon, and evening. Try not to let your dog gulp its food; if necessary, add some chew toys to the bowl so he has to work around them to get the food. Add water to dry food before feeding. Have fresh, clean water available all day but not at mealtime. Do not allow exercise for one hour before and after meals. Following this feeding advice may actually save your dog's life. In addition to this information, there have been no studies that support the contention that soy in the diet increases the risk of bloat. Soy is relatively poorly digested and can lead to flatulence, but the gas accumulation in bloat comes from swallowed air, not gas produced in the intestines.

HIP DYSPLASIA

Hip dysplasia is a genetically transmitted developmental problem of the hip joint that is common in many breeds. Dogs

Dogs need access to water, especially in warm weather. However, it can be very dangerous for a Great Dane to gulp water, considering how susceptible the breed is to bloat.

may be born with a "susceptibility" or "tendency" to develop hip dysplasia, but it is not a foregone conclusion that all susceptible dogs will eventually develop hip dysplasia. All dysplastic dogs are born with normal hips, the dysplastic changes begin within the first 24 months of life, although they are usually evident long before then.

It is now known that there are several factors that help determine whether a susceptible dog will ever develop hip dysplasia. These include body size, conformation, growth patterns, caloric load, and electrolyte balance in the dog food.

Great Dane puppies need to be supervised while playing, as unregulated exercise can put a growing pup at greater risk of developing bone and joint injuries.

in the PennHip™ procedure, which is a way of predicting risk of developing hip dysplasia and arthritis. In time it should be possible to completely eradicate hip dysplasia from the breed.

If you start with a pup with less risk of hip dysplasia, you can further reduce your risk by controlling its environment. Select a food with a moderate amount of protein and avoid the super high premium and high-calorie diets. Also, feed your pup several times a day for defined periods (e.g., 15 minutes) rather than leaving the food down all day. Avoid all nutritional supplements, especially those that include calcium, phosphorus, and/or vitamin D. Use controlled exercise for your pup rather than letting him run loose. Unrestricted exercise in the pup can stress the joints that are still developing.

Although Great Danes are often cited as being prone to hip dysplasia, based on research tabulated up to January, 1995, the Orthopedic Foundation for Animals concluded that 13% of the radiographs submitted from Great Danes had evidence of hip dysplasia. This is great news because the Great Dane breeders have been able to reduce the incidence in the breed by over 20–30% just through conscientious breeding.

When purchasing a Great Dane pup, it is best to ensure that the parents were both registered with normal hips through one of the international registries such as the OFA or GDC. Pups over 16 weeks of age can be tested by veterinarians trained

If you have a dog with hip dysplasia, all is not lost. There is much variability in the clinical presentation. Some dogs with severe dysplasia experience little pain, while others that have minor changes may be extremely sore. The main problem is that dysplastic hips promote degenerative joint disease (osteoarthritis or osteoarthrosis) which can eventually incapacitate the joint. Aspirin and other anti-inflammatory agents are suitable in the early stages; surgery is needed when animals are in great pain, when drug therapy doesn't work adequately, or when movement is severely compromised.

HYPERTROPHIC OSTEODYSTROPHY

Hypertrophic osteodystrophy is a disease of young, primarily large-breed dogs, and Great Danes appear to be one of the most common breeds affected. They are typically affected at a young age, often at three to four months old. The condition is associated with inflammation of affected bones and a derangement of normal bone development.

The cause of hypertrophic osteodystrophy is the subject of much debate. It is thought that an infectious process is most likely, but no organisms have been consistently isolated. Other theories suggest that it may be involved with a relative imbalance of vitamin C, or result from excessive supplementation with

A young large-breed dog is the type of dog primarily affected by hypertrophic osteodystrophy. Rest is often suggested to help ease the dog's pain, but make sure your Great Dane leaves some room on the couch for you!

other vitamins and minerals. Yet others suggest that it is a genetically conditioned defect of bone growth.

Affected dogs experience lameness, often in the wrist areas (distal radius and ulna) of the front legs. The upper leg bones may be swollen, warm, and painful. Affected dogs may experience anorexia, fever, depression, and even simple weight loss. These signs may come and go in an intermittent pattern. The diagnosis is confirmed by radiography (x-rays). Blood panels may have increased serum alkaline phosphatase levels, but calcium and phosphorus levels are usually normal. This helps differentiate this condition from panosteitis.

Because the cause of this condition is not known, there are no specific treatments. Episodes often last a week, and complete spontaneous remissions have been reported. Affected dogs are placed on a balanced diet and often treated with anti-inflammatory agents (e.g., aspirin) and cage rest.

HYPOTHYROIDISM

Hypothyroidism is the most commonly diagnosed endocrine (hormonal) problem in the Great Dane. The disease itself refers to an insufficient amount of thyroid hormones being produced. Although there are several different potential causes, lymphocytic thyroiditis is by far the most common. Iodine deficiency and goiter are extremely rare. In lymphocytic thyroiditis, the body produces antibodies that target aspects of thyroid tissue. The process usually starts between one and three years of age in affected animals but doesn't become clinically evident until later in life.

There is a great deal of misinformation about hypothyroidism. Owners often expect their dog to be obese and otherwise don't suspect the condition. The fact is that hypothyroidism is quite variable in its manifestations, and obesity is only seen in a small percentage of cases. In most cases, affected animals appear fine until they use up most of their remaining thyroid hormone reserves. The most common manifestations then are lack of energy and recurrent infections. Hair loss is seen in about one-third of cases.

You might suspect that hypothyroidism would be easy to diagnose, but it is trickier than you think. Since there is a large reserve of thyroid hormones in the body, a test measuring only total blood levels of the hormones (T-4 and T-3) is not a very sensitive indicator of the condition. Thyroid stimulation tests are the best way to measure the functional reserve. Measuring "free" and "total" levels of the hormones or endogenous TSH (thyroid-stimulating hormone) are other approaches. Also, since we know that most cases are due to antibodies produced in the body, screening for these autoantibodies can help identify animals at risk of developing hypothyroidism.

Because this breed is so prone to developing hypothyroidism, periodic screening for the disorder is warranted in many cases. Although none of the screening tests is perfect, a basic panel evaluating total T-4, free T-4, TSH, and cholesterol levels is a good start. Ideally, this would first be performed at one year of age and annually thereafter. This screening is practical because none of these tests is very expensive.

Fortunately, although there may be some problems in diagnosing hypothyroidism, treatment is straightforward and relatively inexpensive. Supplementing the affected animal twice daily with thyroid hormones effectively treats the condition. In many breeds, supplementation with thyroid hormones is commonly done to help confirm the diagnosis. However, because thyroid hormones affect the heart, and because Great Danes are so prone to the heart disease cardiomyopathy, thyroid hormone supplementation should be reserved for those animals with well-documented hypothyroidism. Animals with hypothyroidism should not be used in a breeding program and those with circulating autoantibodies, but no actual hypothyroid disease, should also not be used for breeding.

INTERVERTEBRAL DISK DISEASE

Everyone has heard of a slipped disk, but some may be surprised to learn that this is a common problem in the dog. Approximately 85% of herniated disks occur in the lower back and 15% in the neck region. The intervertebral disk, like a jelly donut, has a tough fibrous outer layer and a jelly-like inner layer. In some instances, the jelly-like inner layer protrudes or "herniates" through the fibrous layer and puts pressure on the spinal cord. This causes intense pain and limited use of the limbs supplied by those obstructed nerves.

The cardinal sign of IVD disease is intense pain. When a disk ruptures in the lower back (thoracolumbar disk disease), there is paralysis of the hind legs and pressure applied by the herniated material onto the disk. In a very short period of time, the pain subsides as the spinal cord damage interferes with the ability to recognize pain. These cases are surgical emergencies.

When IVD syndrome is suspected, radiographs are usually taken of both the neck and back areas, even when the clinical picture suggests where the problem is likely to be. This is because other areas of potential herniation will need to be evaluated. Occasionally it will be necessary to inject dye into the spinal canal (myelography) to identify the exact location of the problem.

Intervertebral disk disease can be managed medically or surgically, but there are definite guidelines to suggest which is most appropriate. Medical therapy may be adequate when there is mild to moderate pain but no evidence of spinal cord damage (e.g., paralysis). For dogs with thoracolumbar disk disease, paralysis, and loss of deep pain sensation, surgery should be immediate. If the pressure on the spinal cord is not reduced within about 24 hours, permanent nerve damage is likely.

OSTEOCHONDROSIS

Osteochondrosis is a degenerative condition of cartilage, seen in young dogs, in which the cartilage cells fail to develop properly into mature bone. This results in localized areas of thickened cartilage that are very prone to injury since they are not well attached to the underlying bone. In time, when osteochondrosis causes flaps of cartilage to be exposed in the joint, inflammation results. At this time, it is referred to as osteochondritis dissecans (OCD), describing the inflammatory component and the fact that cartilage has become "dissected" and exposed.

The factors that cause osteochondrosis are many, but trauma, poor nutrition, and hereditary abnormalities have all been explored. The most likely associations made to date suggest that feeding diets high in calories, calcium, and protein promote the development of osteochondrosis in susceptible dogs. Also, animals that are allowed to exercise in an unregulated fashion are at increased risk, since they are more likely to sustain cartilage injuries. The fact that OCD occurs mainly in large-breed dogs suggests that the increased weight-bearing needs of the cartilage may make it prone to damage.

Large breeds like the Great Dane are more prone to OCD than smaller breeds. A large dog's weight stresses the dog's joints and cartilage, thus increasing the risk. Owned by Rick and Judy Abrams.

The diagnosis of OCD is often strongly suspected when a young dog of a breed at risk suddenly becomes painfully lame. This lameness may worsen in wet or cold weather or when the leg is extended. Careful manipulation by a veterinarian can usually pinpoint the site of the problem. If finances allow, it is worthwhile to take radiographs of both limbs for comparison purposes. Radiographs should also be taken of other joints on the same limb (e.g., elbow, shoulder) to evaluate for other potential sites of involvement.

The management of dogs with OCD is a matter of much debate and controversy. Some recommend surgery before permanent damage is done. Others recommend conservative therapy of rest, pain-killers, and natural cartilage preserving medications (e.g., polysulfated glycosaminoglycans). Each side has proponents. What seems clear is that some dogs will respond to conservative therapies, while others need surgery.

There is strong evidence to support the contention that OCD is an inherited disease. Therefore, breeding stock should be selected from those animals without a history of osteochondrosis, preferably for several generations.

OSTEOSARCOMA

Osteosarcoma is the most common bone tumor in the dog and is especially common in the Great Dane. The usual picture is one of sudden lameness over a two to five day period, and there may be associated swelling. Osteosarcoma is invariably fatal, and the cancer spreads to the lungs in 80% of cases. Radiographs (x-rays) and biopsies are used to confirm the diagnosis.

The treatment is somewhat controversial because osteosarcomas have proven to be difficult to manage. Amputation of the affected leg is usually suggested if there is no evidence of spread (metastasis). If the cancer is already in the lungs or other tissues, amputation isn't of much benefit. Although osteosarcoma does not respond to many anti-cancer drugs, cisplatin (platinum) therapy has been helpful in cases and may increase the survival time to approximately one year from the time of diagnosis. The genetic link with this cancer has not been established, but since there is such a high incidence in the Great Dane, it would make sense not to breed close relatives of affected dogs.

PANOSTEITIS

Panosteitis is an inflammatory condition that affects the leg bones, and Great Danes are one of the most common breeds affected. The condition affects males more frequently than females and is often recurrent or periodic in nature. Most dogs are less than a year of age, but occasionally, they may be as old as six years of age when first affected. They typically show lameness that may affect one or more legs and may appear to "migrate" between legs. Pain is severe in some dogs, mild in others. Associated problems are lack of appetite, weight loss, and muscle wasting. The diagnosis can usually be confirmed by radiography (x-rays).

There is no specific treatment for panosteitis, but the condition usually responds to enforced rest and mild anti-inflammatory agents (e.g., aspirin). Many breeders recommend the use of diets with lower protein and fat contents, but a dietary role for the condition has not been established. Affected dogs should not be used for breeding.

VON WILLEBRAND'S DISEASE

The most commonly inherited bleeding disorder of dogs is von Willebrand's disease (vWD). The abnormal gene can be inherited from one or both parents. If both parents pass on the gene, most of the resultant pups fail to thrive and will die. In most cases though, the pup inherits a relative lack of clotting ability which is quite variable. For instance, one dog may have 15% of the clotting factor, while another might have 60%. The higher the amount, the less likely it will be that the bleeding will be readily evident, since spontaneous bleeding is usually only seen when dogs have less than 30% of the normal level of von Willebrand clotting factor. Thus, some dogs don't get diagnosed until they are neutered or spayed, in which case they end up bleeding uncontrollably or they develop pockets of blood (hematomas) at the surgical site.

There are tests available to determine the amount of von Willebrand factor in the blood, and they are accurate and reasonably priced. Great Danes used for breeding should have normal amounts of von Willebrand factor in their blood, and so should all pups that are adopted as household pets. Carriers should not be used for breeding, even if they appear clinically normal. Since hypothyroidism can be linked with von Willebrand's disease, thyroid profiles can also be a useful part of the screening procedure in older Great Danes.

OTHER CONDITIONS SEEN IN THE GREAT DANE

- Callus
- Cataracts
- Cerebellar abiotrophy
- Craniomandibular osteopathy
- Cystine urolithiasis
- Distichiasis
- Ectropion
- Ectropion/entropion
- Enophthalmos
- Entropion
- Esophageal motility disorders
- Eversion of third eyelid cartilage
- Glaucoma
- Hemeralopia
- Heterochromia iridis
- Lip fold dermatitis
- Mandibular distoclusion (overbite)
- Mandibular mesioclusion (underbite)
- Mesodermal dysgenesis
- Microphthalmia
- Multiple ocular anomalies (merle)
- Necrotizing myelopathy
- Oligodontia
- Persistent right aortic arch
- Progressive retinal atrophy
- Retinal dysplasia
- Sterile pyogranuloma
- Wry mouth

INFECTIONS & INFESTATIONS

**HOW TO PROTECT YOUR GREAT DANE
FROM PARASITES AND MICROBES**

An important part of keeping your Great Dane healthy is to prevent problems caused by parasites and microbes. Although there are a variety of drugs available that can help limit problems, prevention is always the desired option. Taking the proper precautions leads to less aggravation, less itching, and less expense.

Facing page: Understanding how to protect your Great Dane from infections and infestations before they occur is the best way to avoid problems.

FLEAS

Fleas are important and common parasites but not an inevitable part of every pet-owner's reality. If you take the time to understand some of the basics of flea population dynamics, control is both conceivable and practical.

Fleas have four life stages (egg, larva, pupa, adult), and each stage responds to some therapies while being resistant to others. Failing to understand this is the major reason why some people have so much trouble getting the upper hand in the battle to control fleas.

Fleas spend all their time on the host animal (in this case, your dog) and only leave if physically removed by brushing, bathing, or scratching. However, the eggs that are laid on the animal are not sticky and fall to the ground to contaminate the environment. Our goal must be to remove fleas from the animals in the house, from the house itself, and from the immediate outdoor environment. Part of our plan must also involve using different medications to get rid of the different life stages as well as minimizing the use of potentially harmful insecticides that could be poisonous for pets and family members.

A flea comb is a very handy device for recovering fleas from pets. The best places to comb are the tailhead, groin area, armpits, back, and neck region. Fleas collected should be dropped into a container of alcohol, which quickly kills them before they can escape. In addition, all pets should be bathed with a cleansing shampoo (or flea shampoo) to remove fleas and eggs. This, however, has no residual effect, and fleas can jump back on immediately after the bath if nothing else is done. Rather than using potent insecticidal dips and sprays, consider products containing the safe pyrethrins, imidaclorpid or fipronil, and the insect growth regulators (such as methoprene and pyripoxyfen) or insect development inhibitors (IDIs) such as lufenuron. These products are not only extremely safe, but the combination is effective against eggs, larvae, and adults. This only leaves the pupal stage to cause continued problems. Insect growth regulators can also be safely given as once-a-month oral preparations. Flea collars are rarely useful, and electronic flea collars are not to be recommended for any dogs.

Vacuuming is a good first step to clean up the household because it picks up about 50% of the flea eggs and stimulates flea pupae to emerge as adults, a stage when they are easier to kill with insecticides. The vacuum bag should then be removed and discarded with each treatment. Household treatment can then be initiated with pyrethrins and a combination of either insect growth regulators or sodium polyborate (a borax derivative). The pyrethrins need to be reapplied every two to three weeks, but the insect growth regulators last about two to three months, and many companies guarantee sodium polyborate for a full year. Stronger insecticides, such as carbamates and organophosphates, can be used and will last three to four weeks in the household, but they are potentially toxic and offer no real advantages other than their persistence in the home environment (this is also one of their major disadvantages).

When an insecticide is combined with an insect growth regulator, flea control is most likely to be successful. The insecticide kills the adult fleas, and the insect growth regulator affects the eggs and larvae. However, insecticides kill less than 20% of flea cocoons (pupae). Because of this, new fleas may hatch in two to three weeks despite appropriate application of products. This is known as the "pupal window," and is one of the most common causes for ineffective flea control. This is why a safe insecticide should be applied to the home environment two to three weeks after the initial treatment. This catches the newly hatched pupae before they have a chance to lay eggs and perpetuate the flea problem.

If treatment of the outdoor environment is needed, there are several options. Pyripoxyfen, an insect growth regulator, is stable in sunlight and can be used outdoors. Sodium polyborate can be used as well, but it is important that it not be inadvertently eaten by pets. Organophosphates and carbamates are sometimes recommended for outdoor use, and it is not necessary to treat the entire property. Flea control should be directed predominantly at garden margins, porches, dog houses, garages, and other pet lounging areas. Fleas don't do well with direct exposure to sunlight, so generalized lawn treatment is not needed. Finally, microscopic worms (nematodes) are available that can be sprayed onto the lawn with a garden sprayer. The nematodes eat immature flea forms and then biodegrade without harming anything else.

TICKS

Ticks are found world wide and can cause a variety of problems including blood loss, tick paralysis, Lyme disease, "tick fever," Rocky Mountain spotted fever, and babesiosis. All are important diseases that need to be prevented whenever possible. This is only possible by limiting the exposure of our pets to ticks.

For those species of tick that dwell indoors, the eggs are laid mostly in cracks and on vertical surfaces in kennels and homes. Most other species are found outside in vegetation, such as grassy meadows, woods, brush, and weeds.

Ticks feed only on blood, but they don't actually bite. They attach to an animal by sticking their harpoon-shaped mouth parts into the animal's skin, and then they suck blood. Some ticks can increase their size 20-50 times as they feed. Favorite places for them to locate are between the toes and in the ears, although they can appear anywhere on the skin surface.

A good approach to prevent ticks is to remove underbrush and leaf litter and to thin the trees in areas where dogs are allowed. This removes the cover and food sources for small mammals that serve as hosts for ticks. Ticks must have adequate cover that provides high levels of moisture and at the same time, provides an opportunity of contact with animals. Keeping the lawn well maintained also makes ticks less likely to drop by and stay.

Because of the potential for ticks to transmit a variety of harmful diseases, dogs should be carefully inspected after walks through wooded areas (where ticks may be found), and careful removal of all ticks is very important in the prevention of disease. Care should be taken not to squeeze, crush, or puncture the body of the tick, since exposure to body fluids of ticks may lead to spread of any disease carried by that tick to the animal or to the person removing the tick. The tick should be disposed of in a container of alcohol or flushed down the toilet. If the site becomes infected, veterinary attention should be sought immediately.

Insecticides and repellents should only be applied to pets following appropriate veterinary advice because indiscriminate use can be dangerous. Recently, a new tick collar has become available which contains amitraz. This collar not only kills ticks, but causes them to retract from the skin within two to three days. This greatly reduces the chances of ticks transmitting a variety of diseases. A spray formulation has also recently been developed and marketed. It might seem that there should be vaccines for all the diseases carried by ticks, but only a Lyme disease *(Borrelia burgdorferi)* formulation is currently available.

MANGE

Mange refers to any skin condition caused by mites. The contagious mites include: ear mites, scabies mites, cheyletiella mites, and chiggers. Demodectic mange is associated with proliferation of demodex mites, but they are not considered contagious. Demodicosis is covered in more detail in the chapter on breed-related medical conditions.

The most common causes of mange in dogs are ear mites, which are extremely contagious. The best way to avoid ear mites is to buy pups from sources that don't have a problem with ear mite infestation. Otherwise, pups readily acquire them when kept in crowded environments in which other animals might be carriers. Treatment is effective if whole body (or systemic) therapy is used, but relapses are common when medication in the ear canal is the only approach. This is because the mites tend to crawl out of the ear ca-

nal when medications are instilled. They simply feed elsewhere on the body until it is safe for them to return to the ears.

Scabies mites and cheyletiella mites are passed on by other dogs that are carrying the mites. They are "social" diseases that can be prevented by avoiding exposure of your dog to others that are infested. Scabies (sarcoptic mange) has the dubious honor of being the most itchy disease to which dogs are susceptible. Chigger mites are

Dogs love to romp in the tall grass, which is also a favorite hiding place for ticks. Check your dog regularly and remove any ticks promptly and carefully.

present in forested areas, and dogs acquire them by roaming in these areas. All can be effectively diagnosed and treated by your veterinarian should your dog happen to become infested.

HEARTWORM

Heartworm disease is caused by the worm *dirofilaria immitis* and is spread by mosquitoes. The female heartworms produce microfilariae (baby worms) that circulate in the bloodstream, waiting to be picked up by mosquitoes to pass the infection along. Dogs do not get heartworm by socializing with infected dogs; they only get infected by mosquitoes that carry the infective microfilariae. The adult heartworms grow in the heart and major blood vessels and eventually cause heart failure.

Fortunately, heartworm is easily prevented by safe oral medications that can be administered daily or on a once-a-month basis. The once-a-month preparations also help prevent many of the common intestinal parasites, such as hookworms,

Dogs that play in wooded areas may come in contact with chigger mites, which cause an uncomfortable, yet treatable, skin condition.

Heartworm is transmitted by mosquitoes that carry the infective worms. Dogs do not get heartworm through contact with infected dogs. Owned by Kandi Stirling.

roundworms, and whipworms.

Prior to giving any preventative medication for heartworm, an antigen test (an immunologic test that detects heartworms) should be performed by a veterinarian since it is dangerous to give the medication to dogs that harbor the parasite. Some experts also recommend a microfilarial test just to be doubly certain. Once the test results show that the dog is free of heartworms, the preventative therapy can be commenced. The length of time the heartworm pre-ventatives must be given depends on the length of the mosquito season. In some parts of the country, dogs are on preventative therapy year round. Heartworm vaccines may soon be available, but the preventatives now available are easy to administer, inexpensive, and quite safe.

INTESTINAL PARASITES

The most important internal parasites in dogs are round-worms, hookworms, tapeworms, and whipworms. Roundworms are the most common. It has been estimated that 13 trillion roundworm eggs are discharged in dog feces every day! Studies have shown that 75% of all pups carry roundworms and start shedding them by three weeks of age. People are infected by exposure to dog feces containing infective roundworm eggs, not by handling pups. Hookworms can cause a disorder known as cutaneous larva migrans in people. In dogs, they are most dangerous to puppies, since they latch onto the intestines and suck blood. They can cause anemia and even death when they are present in large numbers. The most common tapeworm is *dipylidium caninum,* which is spread by fleas. However, another tapeworm *(echinococcus multilocularis)* can cause fatal disease in people and can be spread to people from dogs. Whipworms live in the lower aspects of the intestines. Dogs get whipworms by consuming infective larvae. However, it may be another three months before they start shedding them in their stool, greatly complicating diagnosis. In other words, dogs can be infected by whipworms, but fecal evaluations are usually negative until the dog starts passing those eggs three months after being infected.

Other parasites, such as coccidia, cryptosporidium, giardia, and flukes can also cause problems in dogs. The best way to prevent all internal parasite problems is to have pups dewormed according to your veterinarian's recommendations and parasite checks done on a regular basis, at least annually.

VIRAL INFECTIONS

Dogs get viral infections such as distemper, hepatitis, parvovirus, and rabies by exposure to infected animals. The key to prevention is controlled exposure to other animals and, of course, vaccination. Today's vaccines are extremely effective, and properly vaccinated dogs are at minimal risk for contracting these diseases. However, it is still important to limit exposure to other animals that might be harboring infection. When selecting a facility for boarding or grooming an animal, make sure they limit their clientele to animals that have documented vaccine histories. This is in everyone's best interest. Similarly, make sure your veterinarian has a quarantine area for infected dogs and that animals aren't admitted for surgery, boarding, grooming, or diagnostic testing without up-to-date vaccinations. By controlling exposure and ensuring vaccination, your pet should be safe from these potentially devastating diseases.

It is beyond the scope of this book to settle all the controversies of vaccination, but they are worth mentioning. Should vaccines be combined in a single injection? It's convenient and cheaper to do it this way, but might some vaccine ingredients interfere with others? Some say yes, some say no. Are vaccine schedules designed for convenience or effectiveness? Mostly convenience. Some ingredients may only need to be given every two or more years, research is incomplete. Should the dose of the vaccine vary with weight, or should a Chihuahua receive the same dose as a Great Dane? Good questions, no definitive answers. Finally, should we be using modified-live or inactivated vaccine products? There is no short answer for this debate. Ask your veterinarian, and do a lot of reading yourself!

CANINE COUGH

Canine infectious tracheobronchitis, also known as canine cough and kennel cough, is a contagious viral/bacterial disease that results in a hacking cough that may persist for many weeks. It is common wherever dogs are kept in close quarters, such as kennels, grooming parlors, dog shows, training classes, and even veterinary clinics. The condition doesn't respond well to most medications but eventually clears spontaneously over the course of many weeks. Pneumonia is a possible but uncommon complication.

Prevention is best achieved by limiting exposure and utilizing vaccination. The fewer opportunities you give your dog to come in contact with others, the less the likelihood of getting infected. Vaccination is not foolproof because many different viruses can be involved. Parainfluenza virus is included in most vaccines and is one of the more common viruses known to initiate the condition. *Bordetella bronchiseptica* is the bacterium most often associated with tracheobronchitis, and a vaccine is now available that needs to be repeated twice yearly for dogs at risk. This vaccine is squirted into the nostrils to help stop the infection before it gets deeper into the respiratory tract. Make sure the vaccination is given several days (preferably two weeks) before exposure to ensure maximum protection.

FIRST AID

by Judy Iby, RVT

KNOWING YOUR DOG IN GOOD HEALTH

With some experience, you will learn how to give your dog a physical at home, and consequently will learn to recognize many potential problems. If  you can detect a problem early, you can seek timely medical help and thereby decrease your dog's risk of developing a more serious problem.

Facing page: Your Great Dane will love you for life if you know how to take good care of him. Marshall Matt Dillion shows owner Janet DeMaria his appreciation.

Every pet owner should be able to take his pet's temperature, pulse, respirations, and check the capillary refill time (CRT). Knowing what is normal will alert the pet owner to what is abnormal, and this can be life saving for the sick pet.

TEMPERATURE

The dog's normal temperature is 100.5 to 102.5 degrees Fahrenheit. Take the temperature rectally for at least one minute. Be sure to shake the thermometer down first, and you may find it helpful to lubricate the end. It is easy to take the temperature with the dog in a standing position. Be sure to hold on to the thermometer so that it isn't expelled or sucked in. A dog could have an elevated temperature if he is excited or if he is overheated; however, a high temperature could indicate a medical emergency. On the other hand, if the temperature is below 100 degrees, this could also indicate an emergency.

CAPILLARY REFILL TIME AND GUM COLOR

It is important to know how your dog's gums look when he is healthy, so you will be able to recognize a difference if he is not feeling well. There are a few breeds, among them the Chow and its relatives, that have black gums and a black tongue. This is normal for them. In general, a healthy dog will have bright pink gums. Pale gums are an indication of shock or anemia and are an emergency. Likewise, any yellowish tint is an indication of a sick dog. To check capillary refill time (CRT) press your thumb against the dog's gum. The gum will blanch out (turn white) but should refill (return to the normal pink color) in one to two seconds. CRT is very important. If the refill time is slow and your dog is acting poorly, you should call your veterinarian immediately.

HEART RATE, PULSE, AND RESPIRATIONS

Heart rate depends on the breed of the dog and his health. Normal heart rates range from about 50 beats per minute in the larger breeds to 130 beats per minute in the smaller breeds. You can take the heart rate by pressing your fingertips on the dog's chest. Count for either 10 or 15 seconds, and then multiply by either 6 or 4 to obtain the rate per minute. A normal pulse is the same as the heart rate and is taken at the femoral artery located on the insides of both rear legs. Respirations should be observed and depending on the size and breed of the dog should be 10 to 30 per minute. Obviously, illness or excitement could account for abnormal rates.

PREPARING FOR AN EMERGENCY

It is a good idea to prepare for an emergency by making a list and keeping it by the phone. This list should include:

1. Your veterinarian's name, address, phone number, and office hours.
2. Your veterinarian's policy for after-hour care. Does he take his own emergencies or does he refer them to an emergency clinic?
3. The name, address, phone number and hours of the emergency clinic your veterinarian uses.
4. The number of the National Poison Control Center for Animals in Illinois: 1-800-548-2423. It is open 24 hours a day.

In a true emergency, time is of the essence. Some signs of an emergency may be:

1. Pale gums or an abnormal heart rate.
2. Abnormal temperature, lower than 100 degrees or over 104 degrees.
3. Shock or lethargy.
4. Spinal paralysis.

A dog hit by car needs to be checked out and probably should have radiographs of the chest and abdomen to rule out pneumothorax or ruptured bladder.

EMERGENCY MUZZLE

An injured, frightened dog may not even recognize his owner and may be inclined to bite. If your dog should be injured, you may need to muzzle him to protect yourself before you try to handle him. It is a good idea to practice muzzling the calm, healthy dog so you understand the technique. Slip a lead over his head for control. You can tie his mouth shut with something like a two-foot-long bandage or piece of cloth. A necktie, stocking, leash or even a piece of rope will also work.

1. Make a large loop by tying a loose knot in the middle of the bandage or cloth.
2. Hold the ends up, one in each hand.
3. Slip the loop over the dog's muzzle and lower jaw, just behind his nose.
4. Quickly tighten the loop so he can't open his mouth.
5. Tie the ends under his lower jaw.
6. Make a knot there and pull the ends back on each side of his face, under the ears, to the back of his head.

If he should start to vomit, you will need to remove the muzzle immediately. Otherwise, he could aspirate vomitus into his lungs.

ANTIFREEZE POISONING

Antifreeze in the driveway is a potential killer. Because antifreeze is sweet, dogs will lap it up. The active ingredient in antifreeze is ethylene glycol, which causes irreversible kidney damage. If you witness your pet ingesting antifreeze, you should call your veterinarian immediately. He may recommend that you induce vomiting at once by using hydrogen peroxide, or he may recommend a test to confirm antifreeze ingestion. Treatment is aggressive and must be administered promptly if the dog is to live, but you wouldn't want to subject your dog to unnecessary treatment.

BEE STINGS

A severe reaction to a bee sting (anaphylaxis) can result in difficulty breathing, collapse and even death. A symptom of a bee sting is swelling around the muzzle and face. Bee stings are antihistamine responsive. Over-the-counter antihistamines are available. Ask your veterinarian for recommendations on safe antihistamines to use and doses to administer. You should monitor the dog's gum color and respirations and watch for a decrease in swelling. If your dog is showing signs of anaphylaxis, your veterinarian may need to give him an injection of corticosteroids. It would be wise to call your veterinarian and confirm treatment.

BLEEDING

Bleeding can occur in many forms, such as a ripped dewclaw, a toenail cut too short, a puncture wound, a severe laceration, etc. If a pressure bandage is needed, it must be released every 15-20 minutes. Be careful of elastic bandages since it is easy to apply them too tightly. Any bandage material should be clean. If no regular bandage is available, a small towel or wash cloth can be used to cover the wound and bind it with a necktie, scarf, or something similar. Styptic powder, or even a soft cake of soap, can be used to stop a bleeding toenail. A ripped dewclaw or toenail may need to be cut back by the veterinarian and possibly treated with antibiotics. Depending on their severity, lacerations and puncture wounds may also need professional treatment. Your first thought should be to clean the wound with peroxide, soap and water, or some other antiseptic cleanser. Don't use alcohol since it deters the healing of the tissue.

BLOAT

Although not generally considered a first aid situation, bloat can occur in a dog rather suddenly. Truly, it is an emergency! Gastric dilatation-volvulus or gastric torsion—the twisting of the stomach to cut off both entry and exit, causing the organ to "bloat," is a disorder primarily found in the larger, more deep-chested breeds. It is life threatening and requires immediate veterinary assistance.

BURNS

If your dog gets a chemical burn, call your veterinarian immediately. Rinse any other burns with cold water and if the burn is significant, call your veterinarian. It may be necessary to clip the hair around the burn so it will be easier to keep clean. You can cleanse the wound on a daily basis with saline and apply a topical antimicrobial ointment, such as silver sulfadiazine 1 percent cream or gentamicin cream. Burns can be debilitating, especially to an older pet. They can cause pain and shock. It takes about three weeks for the skin to slough after the burn

and there is the possibility of permanent hair loss.

CARDIOPULMONARY RESUSCITATION (CPR)

Check to see if your dog has a heart beat, pulse and spontaneous respiration. If his pupils are already dilated and fixed, the prognosis is less favorable. This is an emergency situation that requires two people to administer lifesaving techniques. One person needs to breathe for the dog while the other person tries to establish heart rhythm. Mouth

If you are going to clip your dog's toenails, you need to know how to stop bleeding if you should clip too short. It's good to have styptic powder handy, just in case.

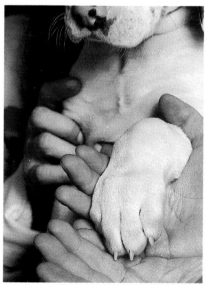

to mouth resuscitation starts with two initial breaths, one to one and a half seconds in duration. After the initial breaths, breathe for the dog once after every five chest compressions. (You do not want to expand the dog's lungs while his chest is being compressed.) You inhale, cover the dog's nose with your mouth, and exhale *gently*. You should see the dog's chest expand. Sometimes, pulling the tongue forward stimulates respiration. You should be ventilating the dog 12-20 times per minute. The person managing the chest compressions should have the dog lying on his right side with one hand on either side of the dog's chest, directed over the heart between the fourth and fifth ribs (usually this is the point of the flexed elbow). The number of compressions administered depends on the size of the patient. Attempt 80-120 compressions per minute. Check for spontaneous respiration and/or heart beat. If present, monitor the patient and discontinue resuscitation. If you haven't already done so, call your veterinarian at once and make arrangements to take your pet in for professional treatment.

CHOCOLATE TOXICOSIS

Dogs like chocolate, but chocolate kills dogs. Its two basic chemicals, caffeine and theobromine, overstimulate the dog's nervous system. Ten ounces of milk chocolate can kill a 12-pound dog. Symptoms of poisoning include restlessness, vomiting, increased heart rate, seizure, and coma. Death is possible. If your dog has ingested chocolate, you can give syrup of ipecac at a dosage of one-eighth of a teaspoon per pound to induce vomiting. Two tablespoons of hydrogen peroxide is an alternative treatment.

CHOKING

You need to open the dog's mouth to see if any object is visible. Try to hold him upside down to see if the object can be dislodged. While you are working on your dog, call your veterinarian, as time may be critical.

DOG BITES

If your dog is bitten, wash the area and determine the severity of the situation. Some bites may need immediate attention, for instance, if it is bleeding profusely or if a lung is punctured. Other bites may be only superficial scrapes. Most dog bite cases need to be seen by the veterinarian, and some may require antibiotics. It is important that you learn if the offending dog has had a rabies vaccination. This is important for your dog, but also for you, in case you are the victim. Wash the wound and call your doctor for further instructions. You should check on your tetanus vaccination history. Rarely, and I mean rarely, do dogs get tetanus. If the offending dog is a stray, try to confine him for observation. He will need to be confined for ten days. A dog that has bitten a human and is not current on his rabies vaccination cannot receive a rabies vaccination for ten days. Dog bites should be reported to the Board of Health.

DROWNING

Remove any debris from the dog's mouth and swing the dog, holding him upside down. Stimulate respiration by pulling his tongue forward. Administer CPR if necessary, and call your veterinarian. Don't give up working on the dog. Be sure to wrap him in blankets if he is cold or in shock.

ELECTROCUTION

You may want to look into puppy proofing your house by installing GFCIs (Ground Fault Circuit Interrupters) on your electrical outlets. A GFCI just saved my dog's life. He had pulled an extension cord into his crate and was "teething" on it at seven years of age. The GFCI kept him from being electrocuted. Turn off the current before touching the dog. Resuscitate him by administering CPR and pulling his tongue forward to stimulate respiration. Try mouth-to-mouth breathing if the dog is not breathing. Take him to your veterinarian as soon as possible since electrocution can cause internal problems, such as lung damage, which need medical treatment.

EYES

Red eyes indicate inflammation, and any redness to the upper white part of the eye (sclera) may constitute an emergency. Squinting, cloudiness to the cornea, or loss of vision could indicate severe problems, such as glaucoma, anterior uveitis and episcleritis. Glaucoma is an emergency if you want to save the dog's eye. A prolapsed third eyelid is abnormal and is a symptom of an underlying problem. If something should get in your dog's eye, flush it out with cold water or a saline eye wash. Epiphora and allergic conjunctivitis are annoying and frequently persistent problems. Epiphora (excessive tearing) leaves the area below the eye wet and sometimes stained. The wetness may lead to a bacterial infection. There are numerous causes (allergies, infections, foreign matter, abnormally located eyelashes and adjacent facial hair that rubs against the eyeball, defects or diseases of the tear drainage system, birth defects of the eyelids, etc.) and the treatment is based on the cause. Keeping the hair around the eye cut short and sponging the eye daily will give relief. Many cases are responsive to medical treatment. Allergic conjunctivitis may be a seasonal problem if the dog has inhalant allergies (e.g., ragweed), or it may be a year 'round problem. The conjunctiva becomes red and swollen and is prone to a bacterial infection associated with mucus accumulation or pus in the eye. Again keeping the hair around the eyes short will give relief. Mild corticosteroid drops or ointment will also give relief. The underlying problem should be investigated.

FISH HOOKS

An imbedded fish hook will probably need to be removed by the veterinarian. More than likely, sedation will be required along with antibiotics. Don't try to remove it yourself. The shank of the hook will need to be cut off in order to push the other end through.

FOREIGN OBJECTS

I can't tell you how many chicken bones my first dog ingested. Fortunately she had a "cast iron stomach" and never suffered the consequences. However, she was always going to the veterinarian for treatment. Not all dogs are so lucky. It is unbelievable what some dogs will take a liking to. I have assisted in surgeries in which all kinds of foreign objects were removed from the stomach and/or intestinal tract. Those objects included socks, pantyhose, stockings, clothing, diapers, sanitary products, plastic, toys, and, last but not least, rawhides. Surgery is costly and not always successful, especially if it is performed too late. If you see or suspect your dog has ingested a foreign object, contact your veterinarian immediately. He may tell you to induce vomiting or he may have you bring your dog to the clinic immediately. Don't induce vomiting without the veterinarian's permission, since the object may cause more damage on the way back up than it would if you allow it to pass through.

HEATSTROKE

Heatstroke is an emergency! The classic signs are rapid, shallow breathing; rapid heartbeat;

a temperature above 104 degrees; and subsequent collapse. The dog needs to be cooled as quickly as possible and treated immediately by the veterinarian. If possible, spray him down with cool water and pack ice around his head, neck, and groin. Monitor his temperature and stop the cooling process as soon as his temperature reaches 103 degrees. Nevertheless, you will need to keep monitoring his temperature to be sure it doesn't elevate again. If the temperature continues to drop to below 100 degrees, it could be life threatening. Get professional help immediately. Prevention is more successful than treatment. Those at the greatest risk are brachycephalic (short nosed) breeds, obese dogs, and those that suffer from cardiovascular disease. Dogs are not able to cool off by sweating as people can. Their only way is through panting and radiation of heat from the skin surface. When stressed and exposed to high environmental temperature, high humidity, and poor ventilation, a dog can suffer heatstroke very quickly. Many people do not realize how quickly a car can overheat. Never leave a dog unattended in a car. It is even against the law in some states. Also, a brachycephalic, obese,

Chester, owned by Stacy Fjerkinstad, tries to beat the heat by hanging out at the beach and shading his eyes with a floppy hat.

or infirm dog should never be left unattended outside during inclement weather and should have his activities curtailed. Any dog left outside, by law, must be assured adequate shelter (including shade) and fresh water.

POISONS

Try to locate the source of the poison (the container which lists the ingredients) and call your veterinarian immediately. Be prepared to give the age and weight of your dog, the quantity of poison consumed and the probable time of ingestion. Your veterinarian will want you to read off the ingredients. If you can't reach him, you can call a local poison center or the National Poison Control Center for Animals in Illinois, which is open 24 hours a day. Their phone number is 1-800-548-2423. There is a charge for their service, so you may need to have a credit card number available.

Symptoms of poisoning include muscle trembling and weakness, increased salivation, vomiting and loss of bowel control. There are numerous household toxins (over 500,000). A dog can be poisoned by toxins in the garbage. Other poisons include pesticides, pain relievers, prescription drugs, plants, chocolate, and cleansers. Since I own small dogs I don't have to worry about my dogs jumping up to the kitchen counters, but when I owned a large breed she would clean the counter, eating all the prescription medications.

Your pet can be poisoned by means other than directly ingesting the toxin. Ingesting a rodent that has ingested a rodenticide is one example. It is possible for a dog to have a reaction to the pesticides used by exterminators. If this is suspected you should contact the exterminator about the potential dangers of the pesticides used and their side effects.

Don't give human drugs to your dog unless your veterinarian has given his approval. Some human medications can be deadly to dogs.

POISONOUS PLANTS

Amaryllis (bulb)	Jasmine (berries)
Andromeda	Jerusalem Cherry
Apple Seeds (cyanide)	Jimson Weed
Arrowgrass	Laburnum
Avocado	Larkspur
Azalea	Laurel
Bittersweet	Locoweed
Boxwood	Marigold
Buttercup	Marijuana
Caladium	Mistletoe (berries)
Castor Bean	Monkshood
Cherry Pits	Mushrooms
Chokecherry	Narcissus (bulb)
Climbing Lily	Nightshade
Crown of Thorns	Oleander
Daffodil (bulb)	Peach
Daphne	Philodendron
Delphinium	Poison Ivy
Dieffenbachia	Privet
Dumb Cane	Rhododendron
Elderberry	Rhubarb
Elephant Ear	Snow on
English Ivy	the Mountain
Foxglove	Stinging Nettle
Hemlock	Toadstool
Holly	Tobacco
Hyacinth (bulb)	Tulip (bulb)
Hydrangea	Walnut
Iris (bulb)	Wisteria
Japanese Yew	Yew

This list was published in the American Kennel Club *Gazette*, February, 1995. As the list states these are common poisonous plants, but this list may not be complete. If your dog ingests a poisonous plant, try to identify it and call your veterinarian. Some plants cause more harm than others.

PORCUPINE QUILLS

Removal of quills is best left up to your veterinarian since it can be quite painful. Your unhappy dog would probably appreciate being sedated for the removal of the quills.

SEIZURE (CONVULSION OR FIT)

Many breeds, including mixed breeds, are predisposed to seizures, although a seizure may be secondary to an underlying medical condition. Usually a seizure is not considered an emergency unless it lasts longer than ten minutes. Nevertheless, you should notify your veterinarian. Dogs do not swallow their tongues. Do not handle the dog's mouth since your dog probably cannot control his actions and may inadvertently bite you. The seizure can be mild; for instance, a dog can have a seizure standing up. More frequently the dog will lose consciousness and may urinate and/or defecate. The best thing you can do for your dog is to put him in a safe place or to block off the stairs or areas where he can fall.

SEVERE TRAUMA

See that the dog's head and neck are extended so if the dog is unconscious or in shock, he is able to breathe. If there is any vomitus, you should try to get the head extended down with the body elevated to prevent vomitus from being aspirated. Alert your veterinarian that you are on your way.

SHOCK

Shock is a life threatening condition and requires immediate veterinary care. It can occur after an injury or even after severe fright. Other causes of shock are hemorrhage, fluid loss, sepsis, toxins, adrenal insufficiency, cardiac failure, and anaphylaxis. The symptoms are a rapid weak pulse, shallow breathing, dilated pupils, subnormal temperature, and muscle weakness. The capillary refill time (CRT) is slow, taking longer than two seconds for normal gum color to return. Keep the dog warm while transporting him to the veterinary clinic. Time is critical for survival.

VACCINATION REACTION

Once in a while, a dog may suffer an anaphylactic reaction to a vaccine. Symptoms include swelling around the muzzle, extending to the eyes. Your veterinarian may ask you to return to his office to determine the severity of the reaction. It is possible that your dog may need to stay at the hospital for a few hours during future vaccinations.

RECOMMENDED READING

OTHER DOG BOOKS FROM T.F.H.

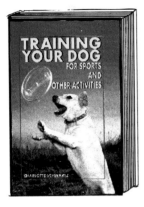

TRAINING YOUR DOG FOR SPORTS AND OTHER ACTIVITIES
by Charlotte Schwartz
TS-258, 160 pages
Over 200 full-color photographs
In this colorful and vividly illustrated book, author Charlotte Schwartz, a professional dog trainer for 40 years, demonstrates how your pet dog can assume a useful and meaningful role in everyday life. No matter what lifestyle you lead or what kind of dog you share your life with, there's a suitable and eye-opening activity in this book for you and your dog.

THE MOST COMPLETE DOG BOOK EVER PUBLISHED (A CANINE LEXICON)
by Andrew De Prisco and James B. Johnson
TS-175, 896 pages
Over 1300 full-color photos
This book is an up-to-date encyclopedic dictionary for the dog person. It is the most complete single volume on the dog ever published, covering more dog breeds than any other book as well as other relevant topics, including health, showing, training, breeding, anatomy, veterinary terms, and much more.

THE GREAT DANE
by Anna Katherine Nicholas
PS-826, 320 pages
Over 200 full-color photographs
Written by well-known dog writer and judge Anna Katherine Nicholas, *The Great Dane* includes practical information about all aspects of owning and caring for a Dane, as well as a detailed history and kennel stories that bring the breed to life. Whether you are a newcomer to the breed or a longtime Great Dane owner and fancier, you will find everything you need to know about the "Apollo of dogs" in this comprehensive volume.